Apprentice
to a
Garden

A new urban gardener goes wild

Evelyn J. Hadden

www.LessLawnPress.com

LessLawn Press First Edition, 2005

An earlier version of "Beauty Is An Opinion" appeared as "The Wisdom of Words" in Northern Gardener magazine (January, 2001).

LIBRARY OF CONGRESS CONTROL NUMBER: 2005909614

ISBN 978-1-4196-1416-3
ISBN 1-4196-1416-9

Designed by Evelyn J. Hadden

Printed by BookSurge, LLC
North Charleston, South Carolina
United States of America

Acknowledgements

This book is dedicated to my grandma, mom, and sister, with whom (until recently) I have gardened all my life.

Many thanks to the other gardeners I've mentioned in these pages, those I know personally and those I only know through their writing, for their contributions to this book and to my growth as a gardener. Thanks especially to my first readers—Kristin, Janice, Sherilyn, and Andrea—for their kind and insightful comments.

Thanks also to my drawing coach, Tim Voigts, for design secrets and crucial motivation.

I am grateful for Alex the cat, gone and sorely missed, with whom I was privileged to spend many happy hours in and out of the garden.

Most of all, I'm grateful for my husband George and his generous love and encouragement.

Contents

Introduction

In this age of nursery-potted plants that can be dug in anytime between first and last frost, in this part of the United States where Spring seems merely a wetter extension of Winter and Fall a cooler extension of Summer, I mentally divide the year into two gardening seasons.

Winter spans the time between first and last frost. It is for resting, remembering, and planning. Except for a pruning day in February and a few mulching days at either end of the season, most garden work is confined to the mental realm, and though physical enjoyment of the garden continues, its sensual effects are starker, more subtle than Summer's.

Summer brings frantic bursts of work spurred on by signs of past work—sweet woodruff's scent, rustling grasses, expanding patches of black-eyed Susans—and noticeable growth from week to week. Uneasy reminders also exist, of errors made, or indecision, or fads gone flat. Summer is a time for reveling in the garden's successes and improving its weaknesses.

This text follows the seasonal pendulum through my first four years of gardening, with digressions to explore lessons learned, in a small urban yard in Saint Paul, Minnesota. Along the way, I've read many books, and I've brought the authors' words into this text to illustrate, clarify, and relieve the tedium of one voice. There is much to learn from books and other gardeners. Yet I've also tried to show that an amateur needn't bend to the great gardeners' rules; each of us has a unique vision, and part of each garden's charm is its wont to reflect the personality and fantasies of its gardener.

The text includes Latin names for the plants mentioned so that interested readers can, with experience or research, envision the plants under discussion. A few diagrams of my garden, an annotated source list, and an index can be found at the back of the book.

The people I mention are real, but events are narrated as I remember them; I make no claim that they are true. No doubt anyone else involved would tell a different story.

A Garden Germinates
(First Winter)

"The task is clear: we need to be awed not only by the magnificence of Yosemite's half dome, or even by the described wildness of the mid-nineteenth-century Maine woods, but by the place we inhabit."

Jim Nollman, Why We Garden

Until my husband and I bought our first house one snowy March, I thought I had escaped the mania that infected my mom and her mom. I was wrong. Mere weeks after we moved in, I started planning a garden.

I read dozens of books, ordered dozens of catalogs, and sketched elaborate designs featuring every element that appealed to me: a pond, a summerhouse, a vine-draped pergola, a tall stone wall surrounding the backyard, espaliered fruit trees, a prairie, a bog, a thyme lawn... all crowded onto a property that measures 40 feet by 150 feet, including the house.

When the snow melted and the ground thawed, I planted two birch trees in the front yard. Then three lilacs and an apple tree. Then two sand cherries. After that, I dug out beds so fast our heads spun. The neighbors' heads may still be spinning.

Why did this obsession strike me in particular? I can only answer that, between the ages of two and six, I lived in Seattle in a house with three backyards. The first was a lawn with formal plantings—an ivied trellis footed by violets, a grove of rhododendrons, a bed of pansies. Behind that stretched the working backyard, with pears, blackberries, rows of vegetables, and a tire swing hung from a giant tree. The third backyard was forested with flowering dogwoods whose blossoms I could only see when marched regally through them on my uncle's shoulders.

That garden is burned into my memory. I spent hours crouched among the plants and animals, my senses inundated and my mind unleashed. And it could have been there, as I patiently waited for a roly-poly bug to uncurl and crawl across my palm on its tickly feet, that the longing for a garden was planted in me.

We moved from Seattle's green-drenched landscape to the subtle-toned desert of southern Idaho, where a gardener's main work was watering the precious plants daily to coax them into surviving. That necessary chore produced amazing results: blueberries we could pick fresh and eat in our cereal, roses blooming profusely against the high chain-link fence, and a nectarine tree so laden every year that, had we not picked the fruits religiously, it would have collapsed under its own weight. I endured the labor and enjoyed the results.

After high school, I moved to Minnesota and a series of college dormitories, then apartments. I didn't think about gardens for years except to show a fond interest in my mom's and my grandma's. I didn't pine for a garden of my own. I didn't even cultivate healthy houseplants; periodically I would acquire a few, which gradually wasted away until I gave them to more attentive friends.

When George and I bought our first house in Saint Paul, I hardly noticed the yard we also purchased, a rectangle of weed-infested lawn barely surrounding our new home. Only after the dust of unpacking settled did I realize how integral the dismal yard was to that place. It supplied the view, or lack thereof, from every window. In front, it served as a ball field for the neighborhood children. In back, where the chain link fence paralleled those of our neighbors and of their neighbors as well, it offered the antithesis of the private retreat that I didn't, until then, know I wanted.

We were living in a vast, barren public park. If we were renting, I would have started looking for another place immediately, even if moving meant pleading with George and forfeiting the security deposit. But our mortgage agreement chained us to the property until selling was financially feasible.

I was placing too much value on privacy, I lectured myself. The neighborhood was in other ways ideal. We had stumbled into one of those rare communities that had managed to hang onto its heart—welcoming new members, retaining its residents for decades, encouraging strangers to converse on the sidewalk—all cemented by a network of regular festivities, friendships, and exchanges of work and child care. Still, I hated being visible to a host of people, even our friendly neighbors, whenever I ventured outside. I hated having to tell the kids they weren't welcome to play on my front doorstep. The need for privacy, the need to impose some barrier between our outdoor space and the eyes and voices of other people, gnawed at me.

I envisioned an eight-foot stone wall surrounding our property, fronted by a massive iron gate. It would inject stability, security, and character; it would cost an arm and a leg. George pointed out diplomatically that it might also send a strong negative message to our new neighbors.

The wall metamorphosed into a less imposing six-foot cedar privacy fence bordering the back and sides, with a short, friendly picket fence in front. Decorative arched gates and a matching trellis with climbing roses would announce that it was a feature rather than a barrier. George shrugged his agreement. I checked prices. We could afford it... in a few years.

We bought the house in March, a dark, gloomy month in Saint Paul. Snow cloaked the ground and Spring was six weeks off. I spent part of almost every day on our three-season porch despite the cold. There I huddled in a beat-up chair and soaked up the sun that poured through the bank of south-facing windows.

I tended to swivel my chair to the left so my eyes could feast on the neighbor's mature jack pine (*Pinus banksiana*) hanging over our eastern boundary, an oasis of green in the gray landscape. From it, my gaze would roam west over white snow and scattered tree trunks and houses and cars, finding nothing worth a pause. I'd turn back to the east, skimming over the bland scenery to linger on the pine, drink up its greenness, trace the arcs of its branches. That tree was the only visible promise that Summer would return.

I thought of my grandma's rock gardens and banks of evergreens, my mom's shrubs and lattices. Their properties might be located in a desert, but even in Winter, they possessed a presence and a stark beauty.

Maybe nostalgia was the final necessary ingredient for the germination of this gardener. One moment I floundered helpless in my landscape, and the next I was thrust onto solid ground as I realized that I could satisfy my own cravings for greenness. I could conceal the houses across the street. Just as my mom and grandma had done, I could paint my own Winter view.

I went to investigate a local bookstore's Gardening section. It was larger and more appealing than I expected; shelf after shelf displayed oversized books, mostly hardcover, many of their bindings green or printed with flowers, so that together they suggested a lush garden at the height of Summer. I drew closer, anticipation unfurling in my chest, and ran a finger along their cool, glossy spines. Their titles awoke more images—The Garden Path, The Undaunted Garden, The Romantic Garden, Stonescaping, Glorious Gardens, Water in the Garden.

Slowly I pulled Glorious Gardens off the shelf and caught my breath as the colorful photograph on the front cover slid into view. It captured the essence of Springtime. Blossoming apple trees arched over a grass path that curved around slim feathered conifers and low pink heathers. This was what I craved, this scene and others as evocative. I spread open the book and leafed through it. Photos enlivened every page, varied in mood and season, and true to the title, all were glorious.

Closing it, I chose several others, then made a beeline for the nearest chair.

The top book on my pile was called Living Fences. From his first sentence, in an introduction entitled "Plants for Privacy and Beauty", Ogden Tanner matter-of-factly expressed my longings. "Is it too much to expect," he asks the reader, "that a house, the single largest investment that most people will make, be not just a shelter, but an oasis, a place where peace and privacy can be enjoyed at the end of a busy day?"

"Yes!" I wanted to scream right there in the bookstore.

He continues: "Why, then, is it that modern building practices make that serenity nearly impossible to secure?" He was writing about our house, set within fifteen feet of taller neighboring houses on both sides, its dining room window looking straight into the kitchen next door, its back chain link fence restricting movement but not sight.

Tanner describes the financial and social barriers to putting up a wall or high fence. As alternatives, he proposes hedges, vines, and espaliers. "The solution is a living fence," he says, "a wall of plants that, with branches and foliage, will screen out views and gently, tactfully, reinforce boundaries."

By the end of the first page, I began to hope that plants could not only enliven our dull landscape, but also increase our privacy. And unlike the fence, I could start adding them as soon as Summer arrived. I bought Living Fences. Then I went home to plan my garden.

First Plants

"I walked into the nursery every weekend the way a friend of mine used to walk into Tiffany's—helpless, her credit card sliding onto the jewelry counter from between trembling fingers."

Amy Stewart, <u>From the Ground Up</u>

When the ground thawed in mid-May, I flipped through the phone directory and called several local nurseries to ask if they sold white birch trees. I love the white birch forests of northern Minnesota. Light and airy in Summer, ghostly above the snow in Winter, their strangeness captivated me after a childhood spent exploring the dark pine forests of the northwestern United States. White birches whisper "Minnesota," and I wanted my little piece of property to reflect its geography.

I also thought trees would be the best way to quickly, dramatically increase our yard's privacy and appeal. Two trees flanking our front walk would gradually obscure the houses across the street during Summer. Bare of leaves, they'd dominate the view with their glossy white trunks, black markings, and strips of peeling bark.

The nursery I chose was about an hour from my house, but it offered fifteen-foot tall birches and a receptionist with a friendly phone manner. As I drove into its graveled lot, I congratulated myself for picking a place away from smog and salt, where the plants were raised in a healthy environment. I hoped my new trees wouldn't mind moving into the city.

I waited on the covered patio while the cashier radioed a fellow to help me select trees. Flats of blooming plants lined the tables just off the patio, but my eyes jumped past them to the rows of potted shrubs, and beyond those to clusters of burlap-bagged trees. A muddy road led out to the trees, and soon I saw a man driving a golf cart out of that improvised forest.

He pulled up beside the patio and asked, "You Evelyn?" He had a rugged face, a gray beard, and a baseball cap.

I smiled and nodded, and he stuck out his hand and said, "Hal." He explained that the recent snowmelt had made a mess of the road, so we'd drive out to the trees. I settled into the seat for my first ride on a golf cart, and Hal asked what kind of birches I wanted.

"Two white birches," I said promptly, though I hadn't known there were other kinds.

"How far apart ya gonna plant 'em?"

I explained about wanting them to flank the front walk.

He shook his head. "Ya don't want 'em touchin' each other's roots or branches," he said. "That's how diseases spread."

I frowned, unwilling to give up my plan so easily.

"Tell ya what. I'll show ya some river birches too. Now those're nice-lookin' trees."

We turned down a side road, past groups of ten- to twenty-foot-tall trees resting on large rootballs wrapped in burlap. A river of cedar chips flowed between clusters of trees and cloaked the muddier parts of the road. I asked Hal to tell me more about river birches (*Betula nigra*).

"They're not well known, and it's a shame. They're not prone to as many diseases as the white ones. Similar look to 'em, but they grow up in more of a vee shape while the whites make ovals."

He stopped the cart near a group of enormous rootballs, each with two or three slender trunks rising from it. The trunks were salmon-colored with brown markings, and they peeled just like the white birches did. They were stunning.

"All right," I said, "What if I were to plant one of these and a white birch, and make them arch across the front walk toward each other?"

Hal beamed. "That'd be good."

"So which one should I take?" I wanted a large tree; I was too impatient to make do with tiny ones.

"If you're goin' for size, don't look at the branches. Just look at how big around the trunks are, and if they have a good sturdy shape."

Hal pointed out a couple of well-shaped trees, and I chose one with three graceful trunks. He wrote my name on a red tag, hopped off the cart, slogged over to the tree I'd chosen, and tied the tag around one of its trunks. Then we backed onto the main artery and turned down another side road, and he helped me select a three-trunked white birch (*Betula platyphylla japonica* 'Whitespire', as the nursery didn't stock the native *Betula papyrifera*).

Nervous and excited, I plied Hal with questions about how to treat my new trees while our mud-encrusted cart lurched back toward the main office. He told me to place them, burlap and all, in the holes, pull the edges of the burlap back from the trunks, then lay several inches of mulch under each of them, spreading it as far as their crowns spread, so they'd have moister root zones.

"They want sun," he said, "But they don't like bein' plopped down in the middle of a lawn. The grass sucks up all the moisture. If a birch dries out too bad, the borers could attack, and you could lose the tree."

Even with the mulch to protect them, the new trees should receive at least an inch of water weekly for the first year, he said. After that, if I kept them mulched, they'd only need supplemental water during droughts.

We left the golf cart at the edge of the makeshift woods and strolled back toward the office through the potted plants. I couldn't resist stopping at the apple trees.

"I ate the best apple last Fall," I told Hal, "A 'Fireside'. I think it was bred in Minnesota."

He nodded. "Yeah, we sell 'em." He showed me the trees and explained that they were a dwarf form, so they'd only grow to about ten feet tall.

I pictured the narrow yard on the east side of our house, where our windows and our neighbors' windows seemed intentionally located to maximize our views into each other's houses. A ten-foot-wide tree would fill that space, and it would bloom outside our dining room window. A sense of unaccustomed power seized me as we picked out a six-foot specimen in a five-gallon pot and set it off from the others. Hal tied another of the red tags around its knobby gray trunk.

I paused again to bury my nose in the fading blue-purple flowers of a potted lilac. The tag informed me that it was named *Syringa vulgaris* 'President Grevy'. Hal was getting the idea now, and he jumped in with his opinion before I could ask.

"This one here's a prize," he said, pointing out *S. reflexa* x *S. villosa* 'James MacFarlane', a three-foot shrub with long oval leaves of dark lime green. It was easily distinguished from the one I had smelled, which bore the typical heart-shaped, dark blue-green leaves. He reeled off its admirable qualities. "Blooms later'n a regular lilac, nice sweet fragrance, and doesn't sucker."

I had to ask what suckering meant.

"That's when they push up new trunks and spread sideways."

It was shorter than the others too, but Hal assured me it would catch up with them in a few years. I tried to hide my skepticism as I examined the plant.

My most recent lilac acquaintance was a huge fountaining shrub in the courtyard behind our previous apartment. It was the only plant in the vicinity that wasn't lawn, and it was a generous bush too, bent double offering its fragrant blooms to all who passed. That smell joyously caroled Spring's return, a welcome message after half a year of Winter.

I awakened one fine Spring morning to a loud buzzing in the backyard and rushed to the window in time to see two guys slice through the six-inch lilac trunks with a chainsaw. Lavender cascades shuddered on the severed limbs as the men tossed them into the back of a truck. Pinned to the glass, horrified, I watched them cut the bush down to a stump, then dig up its great gnarled roots, in less than twenty minutes.

Later that day I encountered several other tenants, and together we mourned the lilac's senseless demise. I couldn't help asking, in my next conversation with our landlord, why he had destroyed that cherished plant. He was shocked by my question and explained it was part of his plan to beautify the courtyard. Two guys showed up soon after that conversation and planted a small tree in the lilac's place.

Remembering the deceased shrub filled me with tenderness toward all lilacs, so I added one 'James MacFarlane' and two 'President Grevy' lilacs to my list of purchases. Then I thanked Hal for his advice and left him to tag these last selections while I hurried toward the office, averting my eyes lest they meet another desirable plant. The woman at the cash register promised they could deliver my new plants and a cubic yard of fresh cedar chips to my house that same afternoon.

I drove home, grabbed a shovel from the garage, and strode around the front yard hunting for the right place to plant the birches. The front yard was forty feet wide. Along its south edge, a three-foot slope rose steeply from the sidewalk that paralleled the street. Slightly west of center, cement steps broke away from the sidewalk, mounted the slope, and flattened into our front walk. I wasn't sure how near the slope the birches could be planted, nor how far from the walk they must be to intertwine above it without strangling each other.

I closed my eyes, trying to picture two full-grown trees where only bare grass lay. In the wild, birches reach maturity after about sixty years, during which time they can grow to seventy feet tall and almost as broad. It was hard to imagine trees that large.

I glanced around. It was important not to crowd the jack pine, so I should probably plant the eastern-most birch as close as possible to the main walk. On the other hand, the birches' roots would need space to knit them solidly into the ground; I should leave a reasonable buffer between trunk and sidewalk. Four feet sounded reasonable to me. A symmetric arch would then dictate that I plant the second birch four feet west of the walk, which meant that their trunks would only be twelve feet apart, but in northern forests I'd seen plenty of healthy birches growing within a few feet of each other. Finally, since I wanted the birches to enclose the garden without shading the interior of the house, I would set them three feet back from the front slope, just far enough inside the property's edge that their rootballs could be buried upright. Decision reached, I began to dig.

Messages bombarded my senses, gone dull from spending the days in the sealed chamber of an office building. My shovel's edge strained against the turf, then broke through its crust and slid into the soft earth below. I grunted and hefted the full shovel, its pleasant weight tugged at my shoulder muscles, and I smelled the rich aroma of fresh dirt.

It thrilled me to hack apart that weedy green carpet. I grinned at the growing pile of shovel-shaped, turf-topped clods. The rootballs on my trees were spheres a yard across, and Hal from the nursery had told me to make the holes at least a foot wider and a few inches deeper than that to encourage quicker spread of the transplanted roots. These would be the largest holes I had ever dug.

After I removed a four-foot circle of sod, I lifted my first shovelful of the dirt under it. The rich, dark, crumbly stuff ended about six inches below the grass, where the dirt abruptly changed character. The new layer was dark yellow, tighter packed, and heavier. Webs of fine gray root wove the top layer together, but the clay subsoil held its shape unaided. This density made it harder to dig, as did the frequent fist-sized rocks that I picked out and piled on the sidewalk.

When the hole was large enough, I hung the hose over the side and turned on the water as Hal had instructed. I started digging another hole while the first one filled. The truck from the nursery arrived just as I'd filled the second hole with water and sunk down exhausted onto the grass to watch it drain. My birch trees lay prone in the truck bed on a mattress of wood chips. Next to them stood the potted lilacs and the Fireside apple. The truck pulled a trailer carrying a small tractor with a scoop.

Three men got out of the truck. One of them mounted the tractor and drove it off the trailer and around beside the truck. He raised the scoop. The other two guys climbed into the bed and wrestled a burlapped rootball into the scoop. The tree sprang upright. It was the river birch.

They drove it slowly up the slope, one man on either side of the tree holding its trunks in place, and lowered it to the ground beside the eastern hole. I had pointed there, reasoning that a vee-shaped tree would infringe less on the square, spreading jack pine, while the white birch could form an unimpeded oval on the western side of the walk.

One of the men asked how I wanted them to orient the tree. Blinking at this further revelation of the gardener's power, I circled the tree to find its most pleasing aspect. The men rotated it accordingly, dropped it into the hole, then held it straight while I heaped dirt over its roots and firmed the dirt with my feet. The man on the tractor drove back to the truck and returned with a scoop of mulch, which we spread several inches thick in a six-foot circle around the trunks.

We went through the same series of maneuvers with the white birch, then the men quickly unloaded the potted plants and deposited the remaining mulch in a pile by the house.

(It was not until the next year that I realized I hadn't pulled back the burlap from the birch trunks, so I dug down under the mulch. A good many roots had pierced the burlap, and it seemed to be partly rotted; I pulled the loose portions of it away from the trunks, then spread the mulch back in place, and the trees showed no signs of suffering.)

I had left the hose running to soak the river birch, and I moved it to the white birch before walking to the side of the house. I had to laugh, looking at that three-foot-tall pile of wood chips and thinking of the cashier's expression when I'd asked if a cubic yard would be enough to mulch my new plants. She'd smiled, her amusement plain in retrospect, and assured me that it would.

I glanced back at my two new birches, their elegant trunks rising from bright circles of mulch, and silently welcomed them to my garden. Then I dragged the three potted lilacs into the side yard, positioned them so they'd throw up veils of green between our front porch and the neighbor's, and again began to dig.

Though sunset was hours away, our side yard was cloaked in shade. The soil was different too, still damp from yesterday's rain, and my shovel sank easily through lawn that was not lawn but a thin mat of ground ivy (*Glechoma hederacea*), which had overtaken many lawns in the vicinity. The locals called it creeping Charlie.

I knew the area only received a few hours of direct sun each day, and lilacs love sun, but I had recently walked with a neighbor through his side yard, passing under a stately row of lilacs whose thick foliage lined his house and shielded his front porch from his neighbor's. His side yard was no wider than ours, I reasoned as I dug three evenly spaced holes in the same relative location on our property. It was a quick job since the lilacs' three-gallon pots were much smaller than the birch rootballs.

I retrieved the still-running hose and dropped its business end into the first hole, and while it filled, I cut the plastic pot away from one of my new darlings and plunged my fingers into its naked rootball, combing and training the fibers, pulling apart tangles. I moved the hose away and let half the water drain from the hole. Settling the rootball into the glistening muddy water, I steadied the plant's slim trunk with one hand, and with the other I scraped dirt back over the edge to fill the hole. I pressed it down with my feet and applied the hose until the mud around the trunk overflowed into the grass and bright tendrils of water lapped at my mud-encrusted shoes. When the three lilacs were planted, I heaped thick mounds of the sweet-smelling cedar chips around the base of each trunk.

I dragged the potted apple tree past the lilacs and further into the side yard and stood it between our dining room bay window and the neighbor's kitchen window, envisioning an airy mass of white-blossomed branches floating between the two windows. Then I glanced back at the lilacs. Behind them loomed the jack pine, loosely filling an area forty feet across, right in the path of the sunlight that breached this fifteen-foot gap between houses for a few hours a day. It occurred to me that our neighbor's lilacs had no tree blocking their midday sun, and a few doubts crept in to threaten my high spirits.

Hadn't Hal from the nursery said the apple tree would grow best in dappled light and a sheltered location? The light was more shaded than dappled, but our house did shield the area from prevailing winds, and my vision of apple blossoms was strong, as was my desire to sit in the dining room and look at something besides the neighbor's kitchen. Banishing doubt, I dug the hole, planted the tree, and mulched it as I had the others.

I wiped my grubby hands on my pants and pushed the hair out of my face. Blood hummed in my ears, knees, fingers, cheeks. My eyes briefly lit on the pile of unused mulch, then darted to the three fresh circles under the lilacs, separated by a foot of muddy ground under which creeping Charlie crouched, trampled but by no means defeated. Its silent challenge stirred me to action. I scooped up an armful of cedar and dropped it between two of the lilacs. Another armful and another, and soon the wood chips were spread several inches thick in a kidney shape that enclosed the three shrubs.

I stepped back to view my handiwork. The ragged edge of the mulch bled into the weed-eaten lawn. Here was a use for those fist-sized rocks I had unearthed during the planting. I laid them along the edge of the mulched area. They stretched nearly halfway around.

I was frowning at the row of rocks in the fading light when two neighbors out for a walk approached to admire the new plants and introduce themselves. Conveniently, one of them offered me more rocks of the same size, which covered a flowerbed she planned to renovate. My eager acceptance startled her—I'd had no idea where to find more rocks—and before she could reconsider, I dashed over and filled my wheelbarrow twice. By sunset, my first planting bed was complete.

So was my surrender to the infant garden.

Gardening in Idaho had taught me to water newly planted trees and shrubs nightly. The task no longer made me restless, as it did when I was a teenager; rather, it soothed me after a day of scurrying and strategizing. Every evening I stood for several minutes at each new plant, hose in hand, and listened to the burbling water and breathed the fresh smell of wet cedar. Gradually the edges of my awareness shrank until I could feel the plants' thirst, sense their roots sucking in the water, and I focused on the exchange as single-mindedly as they did. Water seeped into the ground; tension seeped from my body. The plants' searching roots—and mine—gradually awoke to their new home and began to stretch and taste its offered nourishment.

Greed
(First Summer)

"When I was a little girl, I spent hours playing house. Now I am playing garden."

Dominique Browning, <u>Paths of Desire</u>

My new woody friends had been living in our garden for a couple of weeks when George and I visited a nearby shopping center. In middle of the paved parking lot stood an improvised greenhouse surrounded by rows of potted plants.

"I have to go there," I told George.

He looked surprised, but he followed as I marched across the asphalt, passing up the flats of bright annuals and the tiny potted perennials, until I reached the rows of shrubs. I began stooping to read their tags, most of which held an unfamiliar botanical name and a short list of the plant's requirements.

"I like these ones. Let's get some of them." Startled by his eager tone, I turned. George stood grinning among a group of knee-high shrubs with dark purple leaves. He's the first to admit that his taste is gaudy.

I eyed the shrubs. That color would look beautiful on a blouse, but I wasn't sure how it would look in a six-foot bush. Then I swallowed, reminding myself that "my" garden was really "our" garden, and reached for the tag on one of the little buggers. It said: "Purpleleaf Sand Cherry, *Prunus* x *cistena*. Glossy purple foliage, fragrant pink blooms in Spring followed by black fruit." I turned the tag over and checked its requirements. "Full sun, keep moist until established, space five feet apart, cold hardy –30 to –40 degrees Fahrenheit."

George hadn't noticed my reluctance. "Well? Should we get

some?"

When I first brought up the idea of planting more things in the yard, George did not welcome more potential chores, so I offered to do the planting, construction, and maintenance required by the new garden if he'd help me do the parts that required two people. However, as we'd both be spending time there, I wanted its design to please us both. This meant, I supposed, that if George liked purple shrubs, the garden should have them.

"Why don't you pick out two?" I said. Mixed with a lot of green-leafed shrubs, maybe they wouldn't look so unnatural.

We trotted our sand cherries home, and while George set up the lawn chairs and fixed the drinks, I planted one of the new shrubs midway between each birch and the nearest side of our property, then watered them and spread mulch around them. We sat on the lawn near our young plants, sipped our drinks, and read books all afternoon.

When next I visited a bookstore, I made straight for the Gardening section and sat for hours, paging through photo-packed, pricey books. That time I couldn't resist taking <u>Glorious Gardens</u> home, where I spent many enjoyable evenings sitting in bed with a cup of tea and studying the photos. I dog-eared pages to mark favorite scenes, and in my journal tried to articulate the qualities that drew me to them. I imagined myself into those scenes, examining the plants, touching and smelling them as I did my new shrubs and trees.

I began to notice plants everywhere. In the parking lots of hotels and gas stations, on street corners and in storefront window boxes, and in other people's yards, I saw plants my eyes had passed over before, and I studied them.

Several of my new garden books carried descriptions of common plants. Using them, I tried to identify those I encountered, mumbling their Latin names to lodge the unfamiliar words in my memory. I paid the most attention to shrubs and trees. *Spiraea japonica*, mounds of gold-green foliage with jarring mauve flowers, lined the parkway near my house, flanked by groves of spruce trees. Trees planted by the city—oaks, maples, gingkoes, and catalpas—marched down the boulevards on both sides of the residential streets in my neighborhood. Alpine currants (*Ribes alpinum*) trimmed into rectangular hedges spanned every third house foundation. Arborvitae (*Thuja occidentalis*) abounded, in tall cones and squat globes. I recognized *Hydrangea paniculata* 'Grandiflora', whose mopheads changed from greenish white to rusty pink in Fall. A nearby slope sported a group of Japanese barberries (*Berberis thunbergii*) trimmed in dainty mounds of red and gold. At the end of the block, a lonely tamarisk tree (*Tamarix ramosissima*) adorned a small lawn.

I learned some common perennials too, mostly by spotting them in garden catalogs. Hosta cultivars lined many front walks, while taller borders, usually across the front foundation, included purple and gold coneflowers (*Echinacea* and *Rudbeckia* spp.), mums, lilies, and iris. Garden plots along the alleys brimmed with orange-flowered trumpet vine (*Campsis radicans*), spiderwort (*Tradescantia occidentalis*), and peonies.

Though annuals abounded, I didn't spare any attention for them. I couldn't imagine going through the trouble and expense of planting something that would die at the end of one season. (Later I learned that they can serve useful roles like filling temporary gaps, allowing the space-restricted gardener to try new styles and plants every year, or letting a bed be dug annually to reduce perennial weeds, and annuals that reliably self-sow can even become part of a more permanent planting scheme.)

The rewards of planting and of watching other people's plants fed my desire for more of them. Drawing on plants I'd encountered in print or in person, I began making a list of those I wanted to include in our garden. The list was an odd mix of plants seen but unknown ("tall, skinny, shaggy blue conifer in Ann's yard") and others known from reading but unseen ("*Viburnum plicatum*, striking horizontal branching and clusters of white flowers").

Many of the plants that I admired in books weren't reliably hardy in our garden, which fell into Zone 4 of the cold-hardiness maps shown in the catalogs. Reluctantly, I crossed off Japanese maple (*Acer palmatum*), weeping pear (*Pyrus salicifolia*), sourwood (*Oxydendrum arboreum*), English holly (*Ilex aquifolium*), and a host of other desirable trees and shrubs.

To console myself for these losses, I visited several garden centers and bought some of the plants that made the cut: three forsythias (*F.* x 'Meadowlark') for their early flowers; seven alpine currants (*Ribes al-*

pinum) for the birds, who love their berries; a flowering quince (*Chaenomeles speciosa* 'Texas Scarlet'), which I planted by a forsythia as shown in a photograph in <u>Living Fences</u>; and a willow-leaved spiraea (*S. thunbergii* 'Ogon' Mellow Yellow®) that wasn't on my list but that I loved on sight for its feathery lime-green foliage and mounded shape.

The new plants made my yard come alive. Here and there hunkered tiny groups of twigs and leaves that beckoned me closer. When I watered, or just wandered, I found myself staring at a plant for an unknown span of time, watching it grow, straining to detect the slow breathing that must happen outside the range of my senses. As a child, I'd spent hours in this state of communion, memorizing the faces of pansies, stretching invisible feelers out to the plants and animals around me. I felt profound satisfaction at doing again something that gave me such pleasure, and amazement that I'd made it possible simply by digging a few holes.

By starting the garden, I unwittingly sent a signal that other gardeners recognized; a network of gardeners emerged from among our friends and relations and, to my delight, began offering us plants. Our neighbor Margaret gave me a bleeding heart that came from another neighbor. Devoid of leaves, it looked like a chunk of driftwood, but she claimed it was alive, so I buried it at the northeast corner of the house, and lo, the next Spring it produced a few arches of dangling pink-and-white flowers. It was the first non-woody plant I added to my new yard, which came furnished with a few long-suffering hostas, daylilies, and other prolific spreaders I didn't recognize that grew in the narrow beds surrounding the house.

Margaret and Tad delivered a yellow rose (*Rosa* 'Golden Wings'). I built a cedar trellis over the front sidewalk and planted the rose at its west foot, hoping to entice it to climb. The east foot needed a vine, so I bought a honeysuckle (*Lonicera heckrottii* 'Gold Flame'). As a final romantic touch, I twined a string of white lights through the trellis to welcome nighttime visitors.

Peter and Deb brought over a 'Haralson' apple tree, and Val contributed Italian oregano and half a dozen white lilies descended from the ones his grandfather brought from the old country. I welcomed these contributions with gusto.

When my mom came to visit in August, we walked to the local Farmer's Market, where I was surprised to find several stands selling potted plants. Alongside the usual impatiens and petunias, independent growers sold herbs, exotics, and native perennials and grasses, many of which I hadn't seen at garden centers, and they were priced less than garden center plants.

Mom bought two perennials for my garden, a blackeyed Susan (*Rudbeckia hirta*) and a lavender (*Lavandula officinalis* 'Munstead'), for a dollar apiece. I planted them next to the honeysuckle.

I sat in the grass later that month and watched the tiny black-eyed Susan and lavender stretch their fragile branches toward each other across the mulch. They looked lonely. I dashed off to the Farmer's Market and grabbed up three dozen perennials that I recognized from my reading, then spent the weekend on my hands and knees tucking them into beds around the shrubs and trees. I planted *Veronica spicata* for their spiky purple flowers, *Coreopsis grandiflora* 'Early Sunrise') to honor the prairies that once dominated the Midwest, balloon flowers both blue and white (*Platycodon grandiflorus*) because I wanted to see if their buds really resembled balloons, lady's mantle (*Alchemilla mollis* 'Thriller') because I'd read that its leaves cup droplets of dew and rain, red perennial poppies (*Papaver orientale*) for their fragile petals and fiery color, blanketflower (*Gaillardia grandiflora*) for the butterflies, and an assortment of thymes (*Thymus* spp.) and oreganos (*Origanum* spp.) to add scent to the garden.

In October, anticipating Winter, I worried that we didn't have enough evergreens, so I spent a hefty amount on several three-foot-tall dwarf Alberta spruces (*Picea glauca* 'Conica'). They begged me for an acidic mulch to help them settle in, as they were older and change was harder for them than for their smaller cousins I'd passed over at the nursery. During a rainy weekend, I drove to the nearest garden center and filled my car with sodden bags of pine bark, then spread it at the spruces' feet under the dripping sky.

October ended. I quit adding plants, sure the improved view would sustain me through Winter. The new planting areas, though fairly sparse, gave my eager eyes places to travel, forms and colors and textures to explore. But as I strolled through my young garden, murmuring encouragement that I hoped would last the new plants until Spring, I recalled the quilts my great-grandma used to make from scrap yarn. She'd crochet row upon row of one color until it ran out, then she'd tie on a scrap of a different color and continue. The result was a cacophony of hues, with aqua from a blanket she'd made two years ago fondling the green and pink variegated yarn she used to cover clothes hangers. Hit-and-miss quilts, she called them.

I stood on the front steps and surveyed our new landscape. A row of yellow-green alpine currants extended partway up one side. There were purple splotches of sand cherry here, blue-green forsythias there, vivid swaths of orange-brown mulch, and scraps of greenish lawn connecting everything.

It was livelier than the previous Autumn's empty brown lawn, but it looked like one of Great-grandma's hit-and-miss quilts. Somehow, I expected more.

Growing Dreams

"Like all artists, we gardeners engage in the hopeful work of turning a dream into a reality."

Jacqueline Heriteau, <u>Glorious Gardens</u>

"I think it helps turn reality into a dream!"

Andrea Bell, reviewer's note

During the first Summer of my garden, I spent most evenings outside. I dug, mulched, watered, and stared at the plants, pleasantly shocked that there were so many. Later at night, I tended to curl up in bed with a stack of garden books and catalogs. My favorite pastime was trying on plants—evaluating whether I wanted to add them to my list of desirables.

When I turned off the light after gorging myself on photos and descriptions of possible plants, I mentally searched my garden for places to put them. I tried to envision each of my current babies as it would look when expanded to the full size promised on its tag. It took a lot of faith to believe the plants would grow that large.

Neighbors and friends toured the yard. Their movements were so predictable that I could have choreographed the typical visitor: Stop at the entrance to glance around. Comment on the trellis. Spot something that is blooming and hurry over to it. After inspecting it, straighten and glance around again. Admire the birch trees. Ask about an unfamiliar plant. Start talking about other things.

That fast, the tour was over, and though I continued to smile and chat, a large part of me wanted to keep talking about the garden. Indeed, the ideal visitor would have been someone who asked about every plant.

My disappointment was unreasonable, I knew. I couldn't expect anyone else to love my little plants as I did, or even to notice each one. The truth was, the plants weren't mature enough to be that interesting, but I had started to see them as they might appear in the future. When I looked at the two-foot stick with a dozen leaves, I could see a six-foot cascade of golden forsythia lighting up a corner in early Spring. Most visitors saw only the two-foot-stick.

Once I figured this out, I started trying to describe the future garden during tours. Talking and thinking about it helped me imagine it more clearly. Gradually I began to see not just plants but scenes—how the shrubs and vines in the side yard would metamorphose into a wall of green blocking the view between our house and the neighbor's, how the tapestry hedge across the front would grow tall and dense enough to hide the Woodland Clearing from the street, how the honeysuckle and rose would twine together on the trellis over the sidewalk, echoing the tunnel formed by the birches above the front steps.

I wanted these scenes to be part of a coherent landscape—not with any straightforward pattern to it, but a complex network of views and moods, rich in detail, laced with surprise. I wanted my garden to find its own voice, and I wanted that voice to be as compelling, controlled, and unexpected as a blues improvisation.

As this grand vision unfolded, my doubts multiplied. Were my dreams getting too large for my property, not to mention my budget?

Many of my gardening books were authored by prominent designers, and they focused on gardens that were, to put it bluntly, beyond my means. They discussed "hardy" plants that wouldn't survive in Zone 4. I couldn't duplicate one of their lengthy borders without extending my garden across the street. What they saw as reasonable maintenance demands were for me untenable: vast emerald lawns with crisp-cut edges, oodles of containers packed with plants that required daily watering, double-flowered cultivars that would topple without staking, annuals that must be lifted and replaced twice yearly, bulbs to be dug up and wintered indoors. The authors of these mouth-watering books blithely added rock walls, orchards, and rustic larch-pole arbors as if their space, money, and materials were unlimited.

To ease my doubts, I revisited the bookstore. Studying the shelves of the Gardening section, I noticed books aimed at gardening in certain environments—shade, deserts, extreme northern climates, and most importantly, small spaces. I snatched up several in the latter category. They offered inspiring photos, sample garden plans, chapters on water features and changing levels and maximizing planting space. They offered evidence that small, even urban, gardens could become lush, private landscapes. They offered relief, and fresh fertilizer for my garden dreams.

Most reassuring of all was Joe Eck's <u>Elements of Garden Design</u>, a slim volume that promised to be as useful as its title suggested. The end of Eck's short chapter called "Gardening in Small Spaces" reads: "...although the range of plants grown in a small garden may be limited, and cultural conditions exacting, it still offers one large benefit. For well-designed, furnished with the choicest plants in flourishing good health, cultivated down to its last square inch of space, a small garden can be a perfect jewel, the envy of those with larger spaces at their command."

Those two sentences bolstered my flagging enthusiasm. On the one hand, my garden came with limits, in space as well as budget. But maybe my huge dreams could be realized within these confines. Maybe I could create a small but perfect jewel.

Beauty Is an Opinion

"Being creative means learning to feel good about defying somebody else's sense of beauty."

Jim Nollman, <u>Why We Garden</u>

"Picture how you want to be in your garden," advises Bunny Williams in <u>On Garden Style</u>. "Are you clipping cosmos from a cutting garden? Potting bulbs in a greenhouse? Sitting on a terrace chaise with the *New York Times* spread around you, along with pots of fragrant roses? Dining alfresco in a private woodland spot?"

I pictured myself exploring. Watching the plants grow. Looking for bugs and mushrooms. Hiding. Melting into nature instead of being separated by a windowpane or a slab of asphalt or a haze of smog. I saw myself daydreaming, not spending my precious outdoor time on chores. Though I enjoyed tending to my new plants, I meant to minimize ongoing tasks—the endless weeding, watering, and lawn mowing with which I grew up.

In <u>Outdoor Living Spaces</u>, Susan Frey and Barbara Ellis urged me to think back to the outdoor places I loved as a child, figure out what I loved about them, and design those qualities into my garden. I recalled squatting, mesmerized, in front of a meadow abuzz with insects; lying on a picnic table and watching the tops of trees shiver as clouds tumbled past; squirming into the hidden spaces under and inside shrubs.

I prowled around my one-year-old garden, thinking how it could be improved to foster the activities I enjoyed. There wasn't enough to explore yet. My new plants were interesting individually, but they were too small and separate, like islands sprinkled over a sea of mulch. There should be more surprises. Sylvia Crowe writes: "A garden without mystery is not one to live with, although it may serve as a setting to some great building, to be seen purely as part of a view and not felt as an environment..." I wanted to feel my garden, to interact with it, not just observe it.

There weren't enough animals, either; birds and butterflies visited occasionally, but I had yet to find a caterpillar or a nest. In contrast, the remembered places were lively and diverse communities. Whether forest, desert, lakeshore, mountain stream, or garden, each contained a wide range of plants visited by a motley crowd of humming, fluttering, chattering, skittering, scampering animals.

Finally, there must be more privacy for daydreaming. Some areas of the garden should be sheltered by foliage tall and dense enough to hide those within.

As I would be sharing the garden with my husband George, I asked him the same questions I asked myself. What did he picture himself doing in the garden?

"I'd like to grill, have friends over for drinks, read, maybe hang up a hammock," he said.

I nodded, thinking that I'd enjoy those things too, then asked him to tell me about the outdoor places he enjoyed.

"I like lawns. I like to walk barefoot in the grass," he said.

Dismayed, I reminded him of the neighborhood cats' droppings and the bee-ridden clover.

"Going barefoot," he insisted, "is one of the great things about Summer."

I pictured a close-cropped, lifeless lawn—the antithesis of a community—and conjured up the noisy, smelly lawnmower invading my peace and scaring the animals. In this scene I was no longer lounging or exploring; I was behind the lawnmower, sweating. Maybe I could find another surface that would please George's tootsies but thrive without mowing, a surface that would harbor a diversity of plants and animals.

Then I took a clear look at our neighborhood and began to worry. If I designed a garden in which I could do what I loved to do outdoors, a private place crammed with foliage and alive with animals, it would differ dramatically from our neighbors' lawn-and-foundation-planting yards. Even if my design met with George's approval, it was possible that nobody else would like our garden—not the neighbors, not our friends, not potential buyers.

No, I was being silly. There must be other people who prefer a forest to a lone tree, a thicket to a few bushes spaced neatly as coat buttons, a wind-ruffled prairie to ranks of saucer-sized flowers. I'd read about naturalistic gardens, but I didn't know anyone who had one. Maybe I should meet more gardeners.

When I needed more rocks to complete my first planting bed, Fate supplied them. Now Fate intervened again; the August issue of our neighborhood newsletter announced that a local garden club was forming. I attended the first meeting one evening in a nearby backyard, eight or ten strangers gathered with only a fondness for plants in common.

Our styles and interests couldn't have varied more if we'd planned it. Charter members included a lady who propagated all her own plants, a couple who'd had their complete perennial-packed garden professionally installed three years earlier, a woman who'd transformed half her double lot into a prairie, one who'd replaced her front lawn with terraces covered in creeping vetch and her back lawn with a patio surrounded by Sweet Alyssum, an unwilling shade gardener who lived under a dozen mature evergreens, a novice who'd planted a four-foot by one-foot strip with annuals, a trained master gardener with a stunning wildlife garden who made living wreaths of succulents in her spare time, a woman with a circular lawn echoing a circular deck studded with pots of plants, and me, frantically filling my yard with shrubs and trees.

We met monthly at rotating members' houses, shared dessert during a one-hour business session, then enjoyed a one-hour educational program arranged by that evening's host. Due to our diverse interests, the programs covered a wide range of topics: fruit trees, vegetable gardening, design principles, hardy shrubs, native plants, seed propagation, and so on. During the Summer months, in lieu of regular meetings, we toured each other's gardens, a couple of local nurseries, and a nearby arboretum. Each meeting touched on new aspects of gardening and reinforced our diversity, and it allowed us an outlet for our shared passion.

But two hours a month didn't fill my need for other gardeners' conversation. That Autumn, I wandered into the familiar Gardening section of a bookstore, and because I wasn't dying for photos—the turning leaves supplied plenty of visual stimulation—I pulled a small paperback off the shelf. It was <u>Noah's Garden</u>, written by Sara Stein. Though its only illustrations were occasional black ink drawings by the author, it captivated me just as the glossy picture books had done the previous Winter.

<u>Noah's Garden</u> merges the study of the natural environment (ecology) with the science of gardening (horticulture), and in it Stein explains why a person who is interested in using the garden to learn about nature, who wants to attract animals, and who wants to minimize human effort would do better to avoid chemicals, lawns, hedge trimming, deadheading, raking, and hybrid varieties of plants. It relieved me to find someone who shared so many of my opinions. It inspired me that she had built and championed the kind of landscape I wanted.

Best of all, Stein introduced me to the class of books called garden essay. They favor text over photos, and they offer the authors' personal stories rather than instructions. Like someone who sees the flowers but doesn't notice the foliage, I had ignored these modest volumes in favor of their bigger, more colorful brethren. Now I sought them out, because from their pages issue the welcome sounds of other gardeners' voices.

Garden essay authors share what they've learned about this or that plant—how it holds up in a certain environment, how it pairs with others, if it responds well to a gravel mulch or a pinch of lime or other special treatment. They rave about what excites them. They outline garden projects, successful ones and those gone awry. They ponder in print the garden's influence on the people who tend it, on those who visit, and on the surrounding landscape. Reading one of these gems is like spending several days trailing an expert as she putters in the garden she's built and tended for decades, then sitting down to tea and hearing her philosophy of life.

Though they are uniformly self-assured and self-aware, each author's voice is distinctive. Christopher Lloyd tends to be grumpy and peppers his detailed instructions with snide remarks about lazy gardeners and inept nurseries. Jim Nollman oscillates between mystical and practical, discussing the need to perceive the earth as sentient, then explaining how to make a tincture of calendula. With clarity and grace, Joe Eck distills his experience and other gardeners' observations into the fundamental principles of garden design. Mirabel Osler cheerfully touts the slapdash approach. "The very soul of a garden is shriveled by zealous regimentation," she writes in <u>A Gentle Plea for Chaos</u>. "...A mania for neatness, a lust for conformity—and away go atmosphere and sensuality."

Through the two communities of gardeners that I met—one in person and the other in books—I began to sense the infinite possible forms a garden can take. I began to see where I differ in taste and where I share preferences, and to build a surer knowledge of my own style.

Gradually my worries subsided, and I focused on designing a garden that would please me—even if it didn't match the yards of my neighbors, even if it didn't elicit praise from visitors. And the more books I read, and the more gardeners I talked to, the more convinced I grew that beauty, in the garden as elsewhere, is an opinion.

Spirit of the Garden
(Second Winter)

*"As the seasons pass, recurring slightly differently each year, as gradually
we acquire plants and knowledge from other gardeners, as we unpick our
numerous errors, we have learnt one thing the hard way; it is this: take
other gardeners' advice on design, or accept their plants, only after you
have seen their gardens."*

Mirabel Osler, <u>A Gentle Plea for Chaos</u>

Among the dozen or so piano teachers I've had in my life, Carroll Meyer stands out. It was he who taught me that mere skill does not produce art, that art also demands emotion. He required that I memorize each piece we tackled, for only then could I learn it thoroughly enough to achieve technical mastery. Yet skillful playing was only our first goal; our second was to explore the full range of emotion the piece required.

When I began to learn about garden design, I studied the experts' techniques. I practiced pruning my trees and shrubs for shape, density, and maximum fruit production. I placed and replaced rocks, trying to duplicate the inviting paths in Japanese-style gardens. However, as I developed these skills, I also examined photos of gardens that transcended the "pretty place" category and awakened my emotions—gardens that created moods, gardens that intrigued me—hoping to understand what makes a garden artistic.

The Winter after we bought our house, I set out to redesign our garden. I tried to do it both skillfully and artistically, to follow the advice of experts and to also inject into the design that intangible something that would make it compelling. I started with a most unartistic task: measuring. Most experts agree that, to design accurately from the comforts of bed or desk, the gardener must first measure accurately the boundaries of the yard and the size and location of permanent structures like buildings and walkways. I enlisted George's help for this, which made it quicker and easier; he held one end of the measuring tape while I took notes.

We returned to the warm house, and I drew the outlines of the boundaries and permanent structures on a piece of paper. Then I made a couple dozen photocopies. On one of the copies, I recorded approximate variations in climate. I drew lines with colored pencils to show areas that received a full day, a half-day, and a couple hours per day of sunlight based on my observations of sun and shade over the course of several days. (When I revisited my designations that Summer, I saw how drastically sunlight coverage changed with the seasons and realized that my Winter measurements significantly underestimated daily sunlight levels during the growing season.)

I then drew lines to mark areas with moist and dry soil, which I estimated by poking my finger into the dirt in various parts of the yard. (These rough measurements weren't enough to determine average moisture levels, which vary during the year. I should have measured once a month at midday over a full year to get a feel for the seasonal variation. However, doing the exercise once did help me to gauge the relative soil moisture at different locations.)

I set that annotated copy of the garden plan aside and thought about natural communities. I wanted to create ecosystems, groups of compatible plants and animals that have evolved together, building a web of interdependent relationships. There are woodland ecosystems, prairie ecosystems, thicket, tundra, bog, pond, savannah, and others, but I wasn't sure how to build any of them. Following Sara Stein's recommendation, I ventured into the Nature section of the bookstore and there discovered field guides.

Though most field guides maintain the rift between horticulture and ecology—they don't discuss propagation or garden design—they do outline the major flora and fauna present in various ecosystems. The best field guides describe characteristic animals and plants, explain their known and suspected interrelationships, and sketch the climate and geography that indicate a certain ecosystem. I tried to use that information to figure out where different ecosystems might fit in my garden and what plants would thrive in them.

I sat down with the field guides, the rest of the photocopies, and the notes I'd taken about what George and I wanted in the garden. Then I tried to figure out how to combine all the requirements into one design: the types of communities I wanted to create, the different uses George and I had discussed, and the microclimates I'd marked on the first copy. There were many elements to consider and many needs to juggle, and settling on a place for one element would limit where I could put the others.

I spent evenings hunched over the pile of photocopies, flipping the pages of my garden books for inspiration. Finally I realized there was only one practical place to put the parking area, directly in front of the back gate from the alley, so I carved it out first.

Robin Williams writes in Garden Design that a garden's most important feature is the main seating area, so I tackled the patios next. I wanted to create one in front and another in back, and I wanted both to be private and partly sunny. Several locations met those requirements. In Outdoor Living Spaces, Frey and Ellis suggest sketching several design options at once, so I drew the possible placements of the seating areas on separate photocopies, including the parking area on each of them.

The number of photocopies paralyzed me again, and I had to think about what to site next. I finally lit upon another garden element that we clearly needed: it was important to run a path through the side yard, where damp, trampled grass half-smothered by creeping Charlie oozed with mud after every rainfall. Frey and Ellis counsel that "An alluring path has a destination," so I decided the side path should link the two seating areas, supplying it with a destination at each end.

When I added the path to the photocopies, it was easier to envision the gardens they showed. I added more open spaces connected by secondary paths to the main seating areas; these would be wilder places in which we could watch the animals.

The remaining areas of each design would be planted. I divided them into ecosystems. It was harder than I anticipated. The ecosystems must fit the sun, moisture, and other climatic characteristics of their sites. They also should work with neighboring areas. For instance, I didn't want to place flowering plants that would attract bees near the back seating area where we planned to take meals.

Each ecosystem also has a minimum practical size, and our garden wasn't large enough to accommodate all of them, though I tried to find creative ways to make some areas serve multiple purposes. In one plan, a pond the size of a child's portable wading pool cleverly spilled into the center of a path, which posed several exciting possibilities for crossing it: a bridge, a plank, tall stepping stones, and so forth.

However, I couldn't find a way to fit all the desirable elements into any one design. Those that included a pond left no room for an orchard. I could squeeze three dwarf plum trees in at the edge of the back patio, but only if I gave up the bog.

Generating the possibilities was exhilarating; choosing from among them was heart-wrenching. The extent of each ecosystem and the number of different ecosystems varied greatly from design to design. Each had advantages and disadvantages. The key, I decided, lay in the plants. I would choose the design that allowed me to include the most interesting plants.

Choosing plants could have been another great ordeal. I cast around for a way to make it easier. My solution was to impose a color scheme on each area of the garden. Plants would be screened out if their colors didn't fit my scheme. This shortened the list of possible plants, and I didn't have to worry if they would clash with each other. I'd seen photos of single-color borders in some of the picture books, and I thought the deliberate restraint intensified their moods. A garden with several single-color "rooms" could have a powerful visual impact, if I could muster enough willpower to carry it off.

I had no trouble choosing the colors for each area. Since I spent so much time on the front porch, and since I love yellow, I'd paint the front yard a vivid blend of cream, yellow, and gold to provide a scintillating view from the house. The skinny side yard would emphasize foliage for privacy between the two houses, but I'd lighten its damp shade with subdued pink and white accents, making it enjoyable for strolling. The backyard, the private area in which we'd eat and entertain, would be draped in soothing grays and blues and underscored with dark red to focus our attention within it.

Having made the color choices, I was finally ready to think about the plants themselves. I divided the garden into thirteen numbered areas that encompassed all the possible designs. Each area represented a combination of microclimate, desired ecosystem, desired human uses, and color scheme. On separate sheets of paper, I wrote a description of each area. For the area under the jack pine, I wrote: "Area 1 - dry acidic woodland with dappled shade and layered understory, forming edges of front patio and Woodland Clearing, shades of yellow." Just under the description, I added notes about the types of plants I wanted to add to each area. Area 1 needed a layer of shrubs less than ten feet high to provide shelter and food for birds, as well as a layer of groundcover plants extending under and beyond the shrubs.

On those thirteen pages, I slowly built lists of possible plants for each area of the garden. I started with the list of desirable plants that I'd created during the Summer, trying to fit each one into one of my numbered areas. Then I read through myriad plant descriptions in field guides, appendices to garden books, plant dictionaries like Gary Hightshoe's <u>Native Trees and Shrubs of Eastern North America</u>, and informative seed catalogs like the one from Thompson and Morgan. These sources are rich with data: average height and spread, hardiness, water and light requirements, soil pH preference, growth habit—all useful for gauging which plants will grow where. Some sources provide close-up photos, which along with the data helped me figure out which plants I wanted to live with.

When I came across an interesting candidate that fit the constraints for one of my numbered areas, I added it to that area's list of possible plants. It was slow work sifting through such details, but I enjoyed learning about so many different plants. Since it was Winter and I wasn't spending much time in the garden, the research allowed me to garden vicariously.

After I made a list for each area, I used several books to discover which of my potential plants would appeal to animals. This extra step added more work, but the work would pay off if it brought more animals to the garden.

The most helpful references for plants used by birds were George Harrison's <u>The Backyard Bird Watcher</u> and Carrol Henderson's <u>Landscaping for Wildlife</u>. The latter, written for gardeners in the upper Midwest states, is published by the State of Minnesota. It includes detailed plans for ponds, shelterbelts, and other landscape features best adapted to properties larger than mine, but Henderson ranks many plants according to their wildlife value, which made it easy and quick to evaluate those on my lists. Henderson's book also introduced me to several native plants that I hadn't yet encountered.

Harrison provides fewer specific plant names, but he describes general types of plants useful to birds—layers of understory shrubs, seed plants like coneflowers and grasses, and so on—and he discusses how to arrange the different types of plants and the other elements, like water, that nesting birds require.

To find plants useful to butterflies, I consulted The Butterfly Book by Donald and Lillian Stokes and Ernest Williams, a thin paperback that lists plants used by the most common North American butterfly species during both larval and adult stages of life. The book includes pictures of both caterpillars and butterflies for the 63 species it covers.

I hoped to attract fireflies, but couldn't find a book that listed which plants they used. John Farrand's Insects and Spiders describes their habitat as "open woodlands, meadows, and gardens", which made me wonder why I didn't already have them.

I drew a star next to each plant on my list that was valuable to a desirable animal. The starred plants would get preference when I made my selections.

I read somewhere that every choice a gardener makes about design and materials (both hardscape and plantings) influences the mood of an area, the seasons during which it is interesting and useful, the life-forms that use it, the amount of upkeep it requires, and most importantly, the satisfaction it gives. Therefore, as I tried to settle on a final design for my garden, I agonized over my alternative plans and lists of possible plants. I tried to make my choices keeping in mind what I most wanted: privacy, Winter interest, wildlife, and minimal maintenance.

I finally chose a design that favored larger tracts of fewer ecosystems and would appeal to birds in particular. I waded through the plant lists and, for each numbered area, circled a handful of plants to try first.

Though I was giving up some desirable features and many appealing plants, I felt good about my final choices. After all, my ideal garden would cover acres of land and cost untold dollars and likely never exist outside my imagination. I was proud that my plan would approximate it so well.

When I showed my hard-won design to George, he frowned and asked, "Do you have to get rid of so much lawn?" I was hoping for a different reaction—pride, anticipation, respect for the plan's complexity—and was mightily disappointed. (He's learned a few things since then; now, when I rave about a pond I want to dig, he's likely to say, "Yes, dear, and let's have an island in our pond.")

Eager to find someone who'd appreciate the richness and scope of my design, someone whose encouragement would propel me through the huge effort I was about to undertake, I scheduled an appointment with Michael, a landscape design consultant. For a fee, Michael agreed to visit and discuss our garden with us for two hours.

Two whole hours! It would be the high point of the Winter. Though the garden was hidden under a couple inches of snow when Michael strolled through it with us, I pointed and gestured and babbled as I'd learned to do with garden visitors, describing all the features it would eventually contain.

We came inside after the tour, sat down at the dining room table with cups of coffee, and I laid the precious pages of my garden plan out in front of us. Michael smiled and said, "First, don't plant another thing."

"Pardon?" I thought I hadn't heard him right.

"Not another thing until you've figured out if you can maintain the beds you've already made."

I sputtered, and I am sure I glared at him. The beds weren't even full yet. I wanted the plants to crowd each other, covering the ground to keep out weeds and reduce maintenance. More plants meant less work to me. Suddenly I wondered what Michael's garden looked like.

Michael spoke about the virtues of open spaces and about how I should strive for the right balance between planting beds and lawn.

"Lawn?" I said. "I want to get rid of the lawn. For open spaces,

I'd rather use patios and graveled areas, and maybe a mossy area in the Woodland Clearing." This last was my most recent brainstorm, as enticing to bare feet as anything I could imagine, and bee-free, too. I grinned at George, who was busy listening as Michael catalogued the deficiencies of all known lawn alternatives.

"Gravel beds encourage seeds to sprout," he was saying, "And they require a lot of weeding to stay free of plants. Moss will need to be weeded and cleared of fallen pine needles and leaves. Lawns are much easier to maintain. Unless you want to use pesticides on the gravel every few months."

Of course I didn't want to use pesticides. I wanted to welcome all creatures.

"Then lawn is your best bet," he reiterated, reading the objections in my face. "Patios will give you a different feel, harder and more formal. They don't absorb sound, and you have to worry about plants coming up between the stones. Unless you mortar them together."

I didn't want to mortar them. I wanted patios of irregularly shaped rocks bedded in sand, half-buried by creeping plants, as timeless and irrefutable as exposed bedrock. But I suspected that Michael might not share my deep appreciation for exposed bedrock.

We went through my plan area by area, and I argued with Michael while George looked on. Michael said that I was trying to cram too many things into our small lot. If I expected to spend only five hours a week maintaining the yard, and to be able to leave for weeks at a time during the Summer, I would have to scale it down to a more realistic plan.

"You want something simple, decorative, and easy to maintain," he said. On the contrary, I wanted an engaging, emotion-provoking landscape, and if I followed his advice, I was afraid I would end up with a low-maintenance but boring yard.

By the end of our two hours, I was tired of contradicting Michael's assumptions about what was possible and what would look good, and I was convinced that he hadn't read Noah's Garden. He was no doubt as relieved as I was to say goodbye.

George looked at me dubiously across the closed door. "He made some good points, don't you think?"

"They're only his opinions," I grumbled. "He has a different style than I do."

Years later, I realized that Michael's visit was actually a great help. By suggesting changes and pointing out the problems that he saw, by arguing with my preferences and assumptions, Michael pushed me to recognize how much I valued mood and complexity. Though we had both been talking about how to design a low-maintenance garden, the self-sustaining landscape that I wanted was quite different from the easy-care plantings he had in mind.

That conversation helped me to see why my own design was worth defending. It went back to the lesson Carroll Meyer taught me years before: in gardening, just as in piano playing, what matters most is being emotionally engaged. My goal was a garden that didn't demand much work, but I would work as hard as needed to create the place I wanted: a garden to be not only viewed, but felt.

Gardens Are Four-dimensional

"It is this never-ending cycle, from one season to the next, from one flush of color to the next, from one surprise to the next, that makes me want to go on gardening."

Rosemary Verey, <u>The Art of Planting</u>

Perhaps my garden plans were so ambitious because there was nothing in our yard when we moved in, nothing but four *Potentilla* bushes and a fifty-year-old clump of pink double-flowered peonies. I don't even like double peonies. Their disproportionate blooms, dragging down the otherwise graceful stems and foliage, remind me of the breasts on a Barbie™ doll. (I wonder, could this explain the peony's popularity?)

If you've ever faced a new garden, you know the thrill of starting from scratch instead of reworking someone else's design. No existing structure limits your imagining; the canvas is blank. On the other hand, young plants won't slake your thirst for the shade of a mature tree, the privacy of a full-grown hedge, the eventfulness of an established border.

Gardeners are unusual among artists in that their creations are four-dimensional. Plants not only have width, height, and depth, but they also change over time. Unfortunately, those changes can happen with frustrating slowness.

When I first added my new shrubs, the barren yard suddenly dominated my attention. I spent every spare daylight hour getting to know the new plants. I tried to visit each of them every day, noticing new leaves or stems or berries, comparing and memorizing precise colors and textures and fragrances. Wandering among them, sampling their delights, and communing with them absorbed me.

But when I wasn't physically immersed in the garden, my sensory satisfaction gave way to impatience. At a distance, the garden's structure seemed inadequate and raw, the plants too small, the animals too infrequent, the mulch too bare and bright. I dreamed of an older and more graceful garden, lusher, more prominently framed, hosting an established community of wildlife. I yearned for my property to display the individuality that, in gardens as in people, accrues only with quirks and scars and wisdom, over time.

Time thickens and twists the limbs of trees, paints lichen colonies up their trunks, carpets the ground with bulbs, and knits neighboring shrubs into soft walls. Time adds whorls and craters and cracks and tangles. Age is not distinguished by mere size—compare the fifty-year-old lichen colony the size of a quarter to the fifty-year-old metasequoia eighty feet tall—rather, time has woven the older organisms into their surroundings.

In Elements of Garden Design, Joe Eck uses the analogy of a novel to describe this concept. In a well-written novel, he says, what the characters do and how they end up seems inevitable; being who they are, they couldn't have acted any other way. A garden can exude the same inevitability—as if the plants, being who they are, have interacted with the geography of the place to end up looking exactly as they do.

Perhaps a gardener can hurry along this inevitability. In Shortcuts to Great Gardens, Nigel Colborn offers strategies for hastening maturity; they boil down to setting up a good structure with hard materials, then cloaking it with fast-growing plants while the slower-growing ones develop. The key lies in distracting the attention from what's not there and highlighting what is there.

I stumbled onto this strategy of distraction when I began examining the details of my new plants, an enjoyable ritual that I naturally continued as Winter approached. This made the first full Winter of my garden less frustrating than the previous March and April. Then, the pine tree had provided the only solace in the flat, gray-brown landscape. Now, on warmer days I could mosey up and down the front walk and examine the beginnings of a garden. The shrubs and trees would take years to mature, but their tiny mounds slept peacefully under the snow and their skinny trunks jutted bravely into the white air. The garden was young, I reminded myself, and each year it would become more interesting.

When it was too cold to stay long outdoors, I spent my free daylight hours sitting in the enclosed front porch with my cat Alex. I drank tea and stared out the windows, admiring the decorated trunks of the birches and absently examining every twig and bud that I could see.

That is what sustained me through the season of inactivity and impotence. Focusing on details of the Winter landscape provided just enough fuel for my gardening mania until, freed by Spring, I could plunge back into the cyclone of outdoor observation, weeding, and planting.

The learned ability to celebrate incremental changes allows me to travel for short periods at Nature's pace. It is then that I shift my focus away from the imaginary future garden and truly appreciate my real, four-dimensional creation.

Skeleton Rising
(Second Summer)

"The structure of a garden is what is visible at a distance and what is seen in Winter, when nature has stripped the garden of its flesh, leaving only bones on view. Then, without the distractions of color, scent, and sound, the form of the garden asserts itself. And it is the form of the garden that finally makes it pleasing or not."

Joe Eck, <u>Elements of Garden Design</u>

When the second Summer arrived, I was ready to start ushering my garden plan into reality. I took to heart the advice John Brookes offers in <u>The Book of Garden Design</u>: "What the garden will look like in Winter is the key guideline for your skeleton planting; good evergreen foliage and Winter interest will therefore be the characteristics you seek, and the skeleton plants will usually be sited for maximum effect for viewing from the house." I would use the season to build a strong skeleton in the front and side yards, a frame of shrubs, trees, and hardscape.

My first step was to enlarge the existing beds and create new ones.

A common way to quickly convert lawn to planting beds requires spraying a general weed-killer like glyphosate over the designated stretch of lawn. After it dies, you dig up the dead turf, add soil conditioners like peat moss and manure, and plant. Alternately, to create a weed-free bed without using chemicals, you can pry off the top layer of sod, turn over the first foot of soil, add soil conditioners, pull up sprouting plants every couple of weeks for one growing season, let the ground lie fallow over the Winter to break apart clods, and plant the next Spring.

Both of these methods decrease topsoil, bring weed seeds to the surface, require additives that must be found or purchased, and produce surplus sod that must be hauled away or used elsewhere. The non-chemical method also requires diligent weeding.

Thank goodness there's another approach. It uses no chemicals and is cheaper and easier, though slower. Cover the lawn with overlapping layers of flattened boxes or newspaper ten to twelve pages thick. Top that with four inches of wood chip mulch, then water it thoroughly to paste the whole mess onto the grass, which will eventually suffocate. Left undisturbed for six months, a bed prepared this way will be free of annual and most perennial weeds and will boast a nutrient-rich layer of topsoil created by the decaying turf and wood chips. The technique doesn't disturb existing soil structure or root systems, needs less work than traditional approaches, costs less, converts potential yard waste into nutrients, and uses up those stacks of newspapers that are waiting for recycling day. The drawback is how long it takes.

I like this last approach for being constructive rather than destructive. I used it to make my new beds, but I as I wanted to get my structure in place before Winter, I planted shrubs through the newspapers and mulch. Then I paid for my eagerness by pulling the weeds, especially creeping Charlie, that emerged from the planting holes. But I didn't mind the trade-off.

The new beds expanded my existing plantings into a six-foot-wide border around the level portion of the front yard. I filled this border with shrubs, setting them close enough that they would intermingle in a couple of years. I used shrubs because they would grow tall enough to thwart glances from curious dog-walkers but not so tall as to shade the whole yard, require only occasional pruning, hog enough light and moisture to hamper many weeds, lend structure to the garden year-round, and live longer than most perennials.

The new Woody Border, an informal tapestry hedge, encompassed the shrubs I'd already planted—forsythias, alpine currants, dwarf spruces, spiraea, and sand cherries—as well as the two birches and our neighbor's jack pine. I added several more Mellow Yellow® spiraeas; I adored the original's bright lime-green foliage and thin, willow-like leaves, and the way it formed a tidy, fine-textured globe.

Researching plants for my garden design, I had learned about many shrubs native to the Upper Midwest, and though they are harder to find at nurseries than the standard exotics, I was able to include several of them in the Woody Border. Dogwoods are among the hardiest, most valuable to wildlife, and most beautiful year-round shrubs; I planted several species and cultivars of native dogwoods.

'Isanti' dogwood (*Cornus sericea* 'Isanti') boasts bright red Winter branches, thick greenery, white Spring flowers, and white fruit that birds gulp down as soon as it appears. This cultivar's wild cousins spread into teardrop-shaped thickets roughly six feet high and twelve across. I encouraged mine to do the same by digging up several stems with attached roots and transplanting them nearby.

Gray dogwood (*C. racemosa*) is an understory shrub with light gray branches that fade against snow and greenery alike, but in early Summer it flowers in marked horizontal layers, and after the flowers fall, clusters of white berries grow up from the short red flower stalks. When mine was flowering or fruiting, even frequent visitors would ask, "What is that? Is it new?" The nursery sold it as a ten-foot tree, but during its first year in my garden, a few suckers sprouted from the base of its trunk, and I decided to let it grow into a thicket.

The pagoda dogwood (*C. alternifolia*), on the other hand, would remain a tree. I planted it between the jack pine and the river birch, since it prefers the shade of taller trees. This gorgeous native bears flat clusters of white flowers succeeded by dark blue berries, and its horizontally layered branch structure is striking year-round. It's a good substitute for *Viburnum plicatum*, which isn't reliably hardy in Zone 4.

Under the jack pine, I added shrubs that prefer acidic part-shade. I wanted to make one part of the Woody Border low enough to allow a view out of the garden and across the street, and to let light into the future Woodland Clearing. Since I like the foliage and fragrant cone-like flowers of the native summersweets, I planted five cultivars (*Clethra alnifolia* 'Hummingbird') that only grow three feet high and wide. I also planted four dwarf serviceberries (*Amelanchier alnifolia* 'Regent'), hybrids of a native understory shrub, with white blooms and berries similar to blueberries that proved enjoyable eating for both birds and humans. Their leaves are blue-green, round, and not terribly dense, and they grow up to six feet high and slowly widen by suckering.

I made another bed in front, connecting the Woody Border to the east foot of the trellis, where I'd planted the honeysuckle, blackeyed Susan, and lavender. This bed would be the Butterfly Garden. It cut through the center of the lawn, leaving two oblong grassy areas, each about ten by fifteen feet, that bulged out from the main walk on that side. The bulge farthest from the house would be the Woodland Clearing, in which I planned to replace the grass with pine needles, moss, or gravel. The other bulge would become a rock patio.

I planted two airy butterfly bushes (*Buddleia davidii* 'Black Knight') in the new Butterfly Garden and ran a stepping-stone path across the mulch beside them, linking the Woodland Clearing to the future patio. A person could lounge on the patio, spot something interesting behind the haze of buddleia foliage, and walk across to the Clearing for a closer look.

With the front skeleton in place, I turned to the side yard. Drainage was poor there. Our neighbors complained about water entering their basement, and our drainage spout delivered surges of water that puddled at the corner of our house. This was likely the reason creeping Charlie reigned there; the grass had drowned.

Several of my garden books gave complex instructions for improving drainage by laying underground plastic pipes arranged in fishbone patterns. A few books offered simple suggestions, more to my liking: plant moisture-loving plants like willows and maples to soak up the excess water, or create channels of gravel and sand, which have more air pockets than the surrounding soil and through which, therefore, water will flow faster.

In my design, a path meandered through the side yard past the lilacs, summersweets, and 'Fireside' apple, connecting the front and back patios. I decided to make a gravel channel in the path so it would double as a drainage route, whisking runoff from the narrow side yard to the thirsty Maple Grove in back and the jack pine in front.

There are many possible materials from which to make paths: gravel, stepping stones, pine needles, pavers formal or crazy, wood rounds, wood planks, and more. I chose stepping stones for their informality and Minnesota Yellow limestone because, being indigenous, it costs less and looks like it belongs. I also like its golden color and craggy texture. I laid the stones in a base of multicolored pea gravel, which echoed the fist-sized rocks that edged my lilac bed.

To build a gravel-based path, some books say to lay a subsurface of four to eight inches of crushed rock, top it with two inches of sand, compress that with a roller, and finally cover it with gravel. Other books suggest scraping the ground bare of plants, laying weed-repressing landscape cloth, topping it with an inch of sand, compressing that with a roller, then adding two to four inches of gravel. All this labor goes to creating a subsurface that will keep the gravel from sinking into the soil.

One book mentioned that places with heavy clay or compacted soil didn't require a subsurface. I latched onto this remark, remembering the soggy clumps of soil I'd removed when planting the lilacs, and convinced myself that my path didn't need a subsurface. I could always add more gravel if some of it sank into the ground.

I dug the path two inches deep on the edges with a four-inch-deep channel in the middle. Instead of carting the sod and soil away, I dumped them into the future planting beds alongside the path, creating slightly raised banks, which I rationalized would better direct any runoff down into the path. At either end of the path, I continued the drainage channel into a planting bed, where I dug a three-foot circular catchment basin so runoff could pool and soak into the ground.

I filled the basins with gravel. Then I filled the path, channel and all, with gravel and tucked my trail of stepping stones solidly into it.

I turned the rest of the side yard into a planting area, spreading newspapers and mulch over the remaining lawn on both sides of the path and also covering the gravel-filled catchments. If the path didn't channel runoff as well as a network of plastic pipes, then at least the mulched planting beds along the path would soak up more runoff than the sickly lawn had. Either way, I was improving drainage.

The newly mulched area incorporated the lilac bed, so I moved the fist-sized river rocks from around it to line the sides of the new path. They kept most of the wood chips from sliding into the path. Where the mulched area was steeper, I pounded foot-long cedar stakes into the ground to form short retaining walls between it and the path.

During the next rainstorm, I felt very clever. Instead of pooling under the rain gutter spouts or in the path, the runoff mysteriously disappeared; only the plants and I knew where the water had gone.

I couldn't resist adding a couple of shrubs to the new side garden— an azalea bred at the University of Minnesota (*Rhododendron* 'Golden Lights') that has sweet-scented orange-yellow flowers and long, light green, slightly fuzzy leaves, and also a dwarf hemlock (*Tsuga canadensis* 'Gentsch white') with gracefully arching branches that are tipped with white needles each Spring.

My plan called next for constructing a pergola, six square wooden "arches" that would parade down the east boundary, smothered in trellising and vines. Our house was twenty feet from the neighbor's on that side. A ten-foot-tall trellised pergola would block the direct view between our dining room and their kitchen and gently shelter our side yard from their busy sidewalk.

But the pergola wasn't just a route to privacy. I'd read that tall elements will paradoxically enlarge a small space by drawing the eye up and out of it. I hoped the pergola would transform that skinny passage into an attractive garden room.

There was also the adventure of building it. The previous year, I had enjoyed making the trellis that arched over the front walk. When I first stood with its eight-foot frame towering above me, I felt like I'd given birth to a giant. The thought of building a structure ten feet high and nearly forty feet long made me salivate.

I bought twelve cedar four-by-four-inch posts and twelve metal post-holders, the kind with a square couch atop a long spike. Sinking them into the ground, then bolting the posts into the couches seemed easier work for one person than digging holes, filling them with cement, and setting posts level in the cement. Posts set in post-holders could also theoretically be pulled up again, so a mistake wouldn't be permanent.

I bought a sledgehammer, bolted a scrap piece of four-by-four into the first couch, then pounded it for several minutes until the spike was buried and only the couch remained aboveground. Then I ran into the house and found George, and he helped me raise the first post and held it while I tightened the bolts. I would have to take it down again to build an arch, but I wanted to see how one post looked so I could better imagine the final structure. I wanted to see clear progress.

We were admiring the post when our neighbor stepped out onto her back porch, about ten feet from us, and politely asked what we were doing. I grinned and started explaining my plans for the pergola. The more I raved about enclosure and buffers, the more upset she became. At first I was puzzled, but my puzzlement soon turned to anger at having to defend my garden design again.

I huffed into the house, feeling that caged-animal panic that I'd wrestled when we first moved in.

George came in a few minutes later. More experienced than I in both home ownership and negotiation, he strictly opposed building the pergola if it might alienate our new neighbors. I felt rather defeated until he hit upon an alternative that I kind of liked: I could build the series of arches, but instead of hugging the property line, they could cover the winding path I'd just completed through the side yard. It was a clever solution, and when we showed the neighbors a sketch, they preferred it to my original plan. Some of my enthusiasm crept back.

Nevertheless, I waited until everyone else went indoors before resuming work on the pergola. I pulled up the first post-holder without undue trouble by tying a rope around it and leveraging off the chain-link fence. Then I resumed sinking the post-holders in the new pattern, setting each pair four feet apart and spacing the pairs at six-foot intervals along the path. Wielding a sledgehammer was a great way to let off steam. Several pieces of scrap wood were pulverized as I sank the post-holders, and my stress level went down too.

Next I laid the posts on the lawn two at a time and nailed crossbars and braces between each pair to make an arch. George and I worked together for two evenings to raise the six arches upright and bolt them into the square couches.

Only then did I realize that my next step, covering the sides and top of the structure with trellis, would not be as simple as I'd planned. The arches were not set in a straight line, as in the original design. They now followed a curving path and were set at odd angles to each other. It would take more carpentry skill than I possessed to fit trellis panels to a curving pergola.

What's more, instead of making a green boundary around a romantic secret garden, the pergola would enclose the path in trellis and vines, blocking the stroller's view of the plantings. This tunnel effect might be welcome if the walk were eight feet wide, but my arches were only half that width.

Should I continue to build the curving pergola despite its drawbacks? I thought about discussing my concerns with George and the neighbors. Too embarrassing. I thought about dismantling my work so far, unbolting the arches and pulling up the post-holders and pounding them back down at their original planned locations and erecting the arches again. Too controversial, and too much work.

Perhaps there was an alternative to trellis panels, a material flexible enough to avoid the angle problem and its related carpentry demands. Garden centers sold rolls of plastic-coated wire grid, less sturdy than chain link and about as aesthetically pleasing. The green-colored version might not look too bad, assuming it was strong enough to hold up wet vines.

There was also rope. I recalled several photographs of posts with rope strung between them, gracefully draped in climbing hydrangea or wisteria. I liked the natural look of rope, and a substantial vine would block much of the view into the neighbor's house in Summer, while still allowing a view of my plantings. Maybe I could live with the partial privacy if it meant having a romantic side garden after all.

I opted for hemp rope, a long-lasting natural fiber available in sizes from delicate quarter-inch line to an imposing two-inch marine weight. I chose one-inch rope, sturdy enough to support wet vines and still flexible enough to be knotted around the posts. I could have bored holes in the posts and threaded the rope through them instead of using knots, but I wanted the rope to hang in regular scallops even while parts of it were weighted down by heavy vines.

I calculated the length I'd need to run three tiers of rope along each side of the pergola, then ordered two hundred twenty feet of it from a nearby marine supply store. Several weeks later, I drove over to pick up my rope. The store offered marine supplies, camping supplies, and outdoor equipment of all sorts—hooks, bungee cords, sleeping bags, tents, folding shovels and saws, fishing lures, knives, pouches, tin cups, and more. Ropes of different thickness and material and chains of different link size were wound onto large wooden spools and sold by the inch or foot. My rope, however, came wrapped in a burlap bag. It required two people to lift the bag onto the floor of my car after they'd wheeled it to the parking lot on a dolly.

At home, George and I wrestled the bag out of my car and into the backyard, then I untied it. The rope was coiled inside like a long, whiskery snake. It was exactly the color of weathered cedar.

George has a book of knots. We looked through it to find a knot that I could use on the pergola. We settled on the Bowline—simple, symmetrical, and effective at supporting weight. I practiced Bowlines until I got the hang of them. Then one Saturday I measured off the first section of rope and cut it. The ends started fraying immediately, so I wrapped them in duct tape, which to my eyes wouldn't detract from the pergola's aesthetic appeal. (This is another instance of beauty being an opinion.)

I carried our ladder to the first arch of the pergola, then coiled the scratchy rope around my shoulder. It weighed at least fifty pounds. I hauled my burden and myself up the ladder and tied a Bowline knot around the post, climbed down with the remaining rope, moved the ladder to the next arch, climbed up and tied the second knot, leaving enough slack that the rope hung in a modest scallop. Painstakingly, I proceeded this way along the pergola.

There were six arches. After I'd tied the rope to the third post, I noticed two things: the knots were starting to slide down the posts, and my rope wasn't long enough to reach the sixth arch. By this time, it was dark. I had to work the next day. Cursing the rope and the ladder and the pergola, I abandoned them for a hot bath.

Eventually the ropes were in place. The pergola drew a lot of attention. People would ask, "What's that thing with the ropes?"

I'd explain that it would someday be draped in vines.

They'd say, "That's different." Or sometimes, "Where did you come up with that?" One neighbor kid said our yard looked like a jungle. Another asked if I would get some monkeys and offered to take care of them. The mail carrier complimented me for creating a unique kids' playset, and a friend joked that, like the pioneers, I could grab onto the ropes to prevent losing my way during blizzards.

At the base of one post, I planted a creeping hydrangea (*H. petiolaris*), one of the vines I'd seen gracefully draped along a rope in a photo. Over the next several years, it produced multiple two- to three-foot stems, none of which seemed interested in climbing.

While I waited for it to perk up, I tried the faster-growing 'Markham's Pink' clematis (*C. macropetala* 'Markham's Pink'). It climbs higher than most other varieties and is interesting in most seasons. Its flowers are mauve bells, and it blooms twice a year. After the second bloom, it puts out hairy seed heads that stay on the vine into the Winter.

It wouldn't grow directly up the four-by-four posts; it needs to cling to smaller things like twine or wire. When I guided it up to the first rope scallop, it was reluctant to branch sideways along the rope. It wanted to continue upward toward the sunlight. When I didn't help it climb, it groped around until it encountered lower segments of itself and wound around them. I half-heartedly unraveled it and tried to twist it around the ropes. I'd read about plants sulking but hadn't realized it was such an apt expression. By this time I was sulking too.

I then tried Autumn-flowering clematis (*C. paniculata*). These vines are vigorous, will grow to thirty feet or more, and produce small, white, sweet-smelling flowers in September. Optimistically, I bought two of them. They were slightly interested in crawling horizontally along the ropes, once I helped them start out in that direction.

I researched other shade-loving vines and found one that could wind up the posts on its own: perennial hops (*Humulus lupulus*). Its leaves are golden-green and tri-lobed. Its stems are coated with fine sticky hairs that help it cling; it traveled up the post and out along every rope it encountered. It looked great draped along a swag of rope, too, with its cone-like green fruits suspended by thin stems. It created a screen of foliage, though not a clean scallop like the ones in the books. I was becoming suspicious that gardeners more patient than I had guided those vines in the photos.

During our Garden Club's next annual tour of members' gardens, I spotted a thick vine climbing the side of a garage. The leaves were deeply lobed with elegant curved edges, dappled with white and hints of pink. The berries showed an astounding variety of colors, with blue, white, and pink berries appearing on the same cluster. It was a porcelainberry vine, the owners told me, and it had covered the garage wall in just three years.

Back home, a search through my catalogs and books revealed that variegated porcelainberry (*Ampelopsis brevipedunculata* 'Elegans') is a vigorous vine even in shade, though not as vigorous as its cousin the non-variegated porcelainberry vine, which has become a nuisance in the southern United States. That raised some questions. Sara Stein in <u>Noah's Garden</u> describes how some exotic ornamentals spread into natural areas through bird droppings or wind-ridden seeds and crowd out native species. Would birds eat berries from my porcelainberry vine and drop the seeds in the south? Could those seeds grow into non-variegated invasive vines?

I phoned my favorite garden center, where an employee at the information desk assured me that nothing they sold would be considered invasive anywhere. She explained that variegation was caused by a virus, so a variegated plant could revert to the green-leaved form, but she didn't know if the seeds from the variegated plant carried the virus. She did know enough about bird physiology to assure me that any seeds a bird ate in my garden would drop before that bird hit Rochester, ninety minutes to the south.

Though I wasn't convinced that I'd done enough research, the urge to see my pergola covered in foliage drove me to buy and plant the variegated porcelainberry vine. Despite my guilt over its possible ecological consequences, I was delighted at how it grew. It grabbed onto surfaces with aerial suckers and also twined around small supports. I supplied a plastic-coated wire grid to boost it to the lowest rope, along which it sent graceful branches. I could see that, given more wire grids, it would spread thickly across the pergola just as I'd imagined. When it dropped its leaves in Winter, the woody stems remained twined through their supports like a promise.

And I, exhausted by a season of building bones, gratefully withdrew indoors to refuel on dreams of a beautiful, compliant, and wholly unrealistic garden.

Bare Ground Is Unnatural

"...there is no sport in the world that compares with clearing ground of bindweed. It is far more exciting than golf or fishing."

Margery Fish, <u>We Made a Garden</u>

My garden's skeleton grew a skin I hadn't chosen, a skin dominated by creeping Charlie. This member of the mint family blooms in early Summer with purple, orchid-shaped flowers with dark speckles. The first year, enchanted by the flowers, I let it stay. By the second year, I began to see that those flowers cloak an aggressive personality. Tendrils of creeping Charlie stole under fences and over bricks, traveling underground when necessary, swathing my new wood chips in purple, smothering short plants and climbing the stalks of taller ones. Clearly, its goal was to overrun the garden.

Since it couldn't live peacefully among the other plants, I pulled it up wherever I found it. That good green growth wouldn't be wasted, though; I dropped the pulled plants among the live ones so they could rot and add nutrients to the garden. Weeks passed before I realized that new plants were sprouting from each tiny piece I dropped.

My friend Kristin, also a new gardener, told me that she'd begun weeding directly into a bag. I followed her example and carried a grocery bag as I wandered through the garden, and when I pulled up creeping Charlie, I stuffed it into the bag.

I learned the hard way that I couldn't compost this persistent plant even after it wilted in the bag for days—its corpses would reanimate and take over the compost heap—so I regretfully tossed bags of it into the trash. Its tenacity led me to worry that creeping Charlie might be able to live for months under those layers of newspaper and mulch, and that as they decomposed, it would erupt from the surface like a lake monster waking from hibernation.

However, most of the creeping Charlie in my mulched beds was coming up through the planting holes, and regular pulling seemed to kill it off. In the future, I hoped I'd have the patience to let the newspapers and mulch lie for six months doing their job of transforming weeds into rich soil.

Within a season, I reduced my creeping Charlie weeding to the errant strands that slithered into the planting beds from the neighboring lawn. Unfortunately, the best times to weed are during its Spring and Fall flowering, and I had to force myself to yank out each strand of green decorated with gorgeous purple blooms.

Though the pretty strands pulled easily from the mulch, those rooted in the compacted lawn tended to break in my hand, and the remaining ends redoubled their growth through the lawn. I didn't want to use chemicals to kill it; I wasn't sure they'd work, and I didn't want to risk hurting the nearby shrub and tree roots.

In case our lawn was simply too shaded to stand up against interlopers, I bought a box of shade-tolerant grass seed (mostly mixed sedges) to boost its strength. One weekend I pulled all the creeping Charlie that I could find, then spread the seed thickly over the bare spots. Before the season passed, the lawn returned to its previous infested state.

Though I don't care for lawns, my sympathies lay with the grasses. They were forced into an unhealthy environment—routinely chopped and prevented from reseeding, shaded into a torpor, smothered and burnt by acidic pine needles. No wonder they lacked the energy to defend their territory.

However, I couldn't allow the lawn's slow strangulation to ruin my garden. I resolved to replace it in the next few years. Meanwhile, I kept weeding.

The other common weed that troubled my yard was the dandelion (*Taraxacum officinale*). Their shaggy flowers cheered me, and I wouldn't have minded leaving them to proliferate in peace, but while there were lawns nearby, any dandelion that went to seed must be considered a menace if I didn't want to spur my neighbors to use more weed-killing chemicals.

Conventional wisdom decrees that dandelions must be dug out. Always on the lookout for more efficient ways to do things (and, you guessed it, save myself some work), I was excited to read about a different method. In <u>Bringing a Garden to Life</u>, Carol Williams writes: "No plant can survive indefinitely without leaves, so if one keeps hoeing off the tops the plant will, eventually, lose its will to live."

Though she warns that this approach won't work for every plant, I decided to try it on my dandelions. It did not noticeably decrease their vigor. When I pulled off their leaves, they grew new ones. Gertrude Jekyl apparently wrote the truth in 1908: "And it is no use just to pull off the top."

However, it was useful to pull off their buds and flowers to prevent their setting seed, and this I tried to do faithfully. My boulevard lawn, just for doing it, looked markedly greener than the neighbors' lawns, in which dandelions were free to seed between mowings.

But plucking the flowers was a temporary measure. Unless I wanted to apply chemicals, I would have to dig those plants out. I started doing a few every time I went out with a spade, and I continued to pluck the flowers whenever I saw them.

I discovered that I couldn't drop severed flowers or even buds onto the ground; given a few days, they often summoned a burst of stored energy and went to seed. I had to add dandelion heads to the creeping Charlie pieces in the weed bag I carried around the garden.

My grandma happened to be visiting one Spring when the dandelions were in full flower, before I'd dug up many but after I'd figured out that I should pick off their flowers. Grandma enjoyed yard work and liked to keep busy even on vacations, so I sent her off with a two-gallon plastic bag to pick dandelion heads. After half an hour, she came back inside the house.

"I filled the bag," she said. "Do you have anything bigger?"

I raised my brows, surprised that my little lawn contained so many dandelions, and fished a ten-gallon plastic garbage bag out from under the kitchen sink and handed it to her.

"Thanks." She waved and was gone before I could tell her not to work too hard.

Another hour passed. She came back for a second garbage bag. I had to go out and see the first one to believe it. It was filled, sides bulging. "Are you only picking off their heads?" I asked. "You're not pulling them up, are you?"

"Just doing their heads." She snatched the garbage bag and dashed back to the boulevard.

The neighbors (who do notice such things) must have thought I was a slave driver, lounging in the house all afternoon while my poor grandma plucked the heads off my dandelions. I felt guilty for handing over such a large job. She would never stop in the middle of it, either. She relished challenges, and she'd clearly developed a vendetta for those dandelions.

The second garbage bag was three-quarters full when she returned to the house victorious. I thanked her profusely and watched her kick off her shoes and sink onto the couch, and I knew that before her next visit, I would have to dig up all those dandelions.

My third main weed grew in several of the shadiest narrow beds along the house, had a long stalk of clear lavender bell-shaped flowers, and bloomed from mid-Summer through late August. I found a photo of it in the White Flower Farm catalog, labeled as ladybells (*Adenophora confusa*). The catalog said only a botanist could distinguish it from creeping bell-flower (*Campanula ranunculoides*). Once I got to know my plants better, I decided they must be creeping bellflower, but by then I'd called them ladybells for too long to change.

Whatever the name, I loved the flowers and thought they'd look beautiful shooting up from between the lime-green spiraeas in front. So in early Fall, when my ladybells developed hard round seed pods up and down their stems, I shook a few of the dried stalks over the new bushes, letting seed rattle to the ground and hoping a few purple flowerstalks would appear the next year.

The next year, ladybells grew up in a huge cluster where I'd shaken the seeds. They must have loved the garden soil, which was richer in nutrients and water than the dry dust under the eaves where they'd been struggling. There were more than I'd expected, so I pulled a lot of the stalks before they went to seed, but the few that were left expanded the next year, drastically increasing their numbers and nearly smothering a nearby spiraea. Since shrub welfare was my top priority, I yanked up all the ladybells in the area. I'd have to find another pretty flower to live among the spiraeas.

Perhaps because I'd successfully subdued the creeping Charlie, I was willing to risk the ladybells in another part of the garden. I shook a few seeds into the opposite corner of the front yard, where several ambitious clumps of daylilies prepared to take over a piece of open ground surrounded by forsythia, sand cherry, and dogwood shrubs. Those shrubs were close to six feet tall and impervious to attack, and though I'm not usually bloodthirsty, I thought it might be interesting to watch the daylilies and ladybells fight over the territory. Call it scientific curiosity.

The next year, I was still trying to banish the ladybells from the first area in which I'd sown them. Not only do they self-sow prolifically every Summer, they also push up new plants from running roots. Add to this an ingenious quick-release mechanism that I discovered by digging down past the running roots. These shallow roots attach by thin filaments to a deep, fleshy taproot. No matter how gently I pulled, the filaments broke and left the taproot undisturbed. To remove ladybells would mean digging up every taproot, which could damage the roots of nearby shrubs and trees.

I began to suspect that, in Minnesota at least, bare ground is unnatural. Creeping Charlie, dandelions, and ladybells were the old-timers, long-term residents of my property fighting to keep their territory, but they weren't the only threats to bare ground. Other plants showed up uninvited, newcomers seeking to stake claims.

Though I was skittish about welcoming another possible thug, curiosity wouldn't let me snuff out unknown volunteers without getting acquainted first. I hated to reject plants that were suited to the environment. The garden was still relatively bare, and there was room for volunteers that could mix happily with my chosen inhabitants.

I removed all but a few specimens of each new arrival. Then I waited, and during the growing season tried to decide whether to fight them or let them stay.

Two of the newcomers arrived as seeds in some mulch—not the cedar wood chips from the nursery, but free chipped wood that any resident can pick up from a county distribution center.

My plans required a lot of wood chips, and I didn't mind transporting them if they were free. The process wasn't messy once my friend Kristin showed me how to make a mulch burrito.

You need a tarp (ten by twelve feet is about the right size for me) and a bucket. Back up to the pile of wood chips, open the trunk, and stretch the tarp across it, leaving extra tarp hanging out on all sides. Use the bucket to scoop wood chips into the cavity, and when it is full, fold the edges of the tarp around their mulch "filling". This keeps wood bits, bugs, and sap off the trunk carpet and reduces cleanup to nearly nothing.

After using the bucket to unload the first few wheelbarrows-full of wood chips, I lift the remainder and bundle it, tarp and all, into the wheelbarrow, cart it to the bed I am covering, and tip it onto the ground. When I pull the tarp clear and shake it out, cleanup is done.

Using the mulch burrito technique, I covered my new planting beds with free mulch and topped off the previous year's cedar chips with it as well. Soon, up from the mulch sprouted a vining plant with loose sprays of white flowers, and a plant with a prickly clump of oval leaves and a tall stem that supported clusters of tiny yellow flowers. John and Evelyn Moyle identify the first as fringed bindweed (*Polygonum cilinode*) in Northland Wild Flowers. After a season of observation, I decided to let it stay under the jack pine as long as it didn't strangle any ladyferns and didn't spread fast enough to scare me.

I consulted several books but couldn't identify the yellow-flowered plant. However, I noticed that it attracted cabbage white butterflies. According to The Butterfly Book by Stokes, Stokes, and Williams, cabbage whites often choose mustard species for food and egg-laying. I looked up mustards in a field guide and guessed that my plant was black mustard (*Brassica nigra*). Even though it and the other brassicas are considered agricultural weeds, I decided to keep it in the Butterfly Garden for the cabbage whites. Since it's an annual, I figured I could control it by pulling seedlings every Spring.

Also up from the mulch grew a plant that looked suspiciously like catnip (*Nepeta cataria*), and whose placement, when I thought about it, coincided with deposits from neighborhood cats. My own cat, Alex, confirmed that it was a delicacy, so I moved it to the backyard, hoping to establish a private stash. I ended up planting more catnip seeds because Alex quickly decimated the initial population. With him on catnip patrol, this rampant herb would not overrun my garden.

In sunny areas where the soil was moist enough, there grew an intriguing plant with a loose structure of stems and a few long pointed leaves. Its flowers were inch-long cones coated with pink and white kernels. The plants tended to be a couple of feet tall and wide, except for the few that made it into the tomato patch and greedily partook of the rich soil. They were easy to identify as dock-leaved smartweed (*Polygonum lapathifolium*), an annual that the Moyles' book informed me enjoys "damp soils subject to flooding". The flowers remind me of the pink and white candy-coated licorice pieces, whose names I can't remember, that my sister and I bought at movie theaters when we were children. I wanted to keep smartweed around for this memory, so I let it stay and self-sow in two of the places it had chosen.

A horde of tiny treelings volunteered in the new garden as well, from seeds blown in by the wind or buried by squirrels the previous Fall. They sprouted under the skirts of other plants and between the legs of the shrubs, camouflaged against casual notice. I would have liked to watch some of them grow to maturity, but I had to pull them. There was no more space for trees, especially self-sowers, in my small garden.

I began to wonder if Michael the landscape consultant was right to caution me about creating so many planting areas. Uninvited plants were moving in while I wasn't looking. The unwanted ones were spreading faster than I could stop them. And I didn't want to work that hard.

Some gardeners seem to enjoy the grim battle against unwanted plants; they stand ready with a hoe or an arsenal of pest-deterring chemicals, spurred on by the challenge of human against Nature. I, however, crave peace.

Even if I managed to pull all my current weeds, I knew I couldn't prevent wind, birds, or squirrels bringing new ones every season. And I was willing to work to create the garden I'd designed. But for it to become the self-sustaining landscape that I envisioned, the amount of weeding would have to shrink dramatically.

Deciding whether to keep each of my volunteers taught me that, to keep maintenance low, I needed to know the plants' reproductive strategies. I made some lucky initial choices in that respect. I chose shrubs, and mostly non-suckering types, to provide the framework of the garden. Those that did sucker were free to mingle in the Woody Border; my main job was to watch that none of them strangled its neighbors.

Most of my perennials didn't self-sow. Perhaps the mulch deterred them. I used many of these—lady's mantle, hosta, miniature goatsbeard (*Aruncus aethusifolius*), lavender—along the edges of plantings because they were less likely to invade the lawn yet dense enough to keep from being invaded. It was a relief, too, that they grew in manageable mounds and stayed where I put them.

Other perennials produced one or two new plants in their general vicinity each year—rock cress (*Arabis caucasica*), heuchera, and cushion spurge (*Euphorbia polychroma*). The seedlings were welcome at that early stage of my garden. Eventually the beds might be too full for new seedlings, but I would enjoy offering them to gardening friends.

Still other perennials self-sowed heartily—blackeyed Susans (the species *Rudbeckia hirta* but, curiously, not *R. fulgida* var. *sullivantii* 'Goldsturm', which produced no seedlings), a double-flowered strain of feverfew (*Tanacetum parthenium*), and *Coreopsis grandiflora* 'Early Sunrise'. I'd have to judge the work against their value, but for now, I gratefully used the seedlings to fill gaps.

Several of the perennials I planted in the side garden—columbines (*Aquilegia hybrida* 'Nora Barlow'), forget-me-nots (*Myosotis* cultivars), and lady's smock (*Cardamine pratensis*)—surprised me by self-sowing thickly in the gravel path, proving that Michael the consultant was right about its maintenance requirements. I was only too eager to move these seedlings into the sparsely planted beds, where they could spread with my blessing.

I was starting to appreciate that extra plants were a gardener's currency and was looking forward to having some to give away. The gardeners that I knew were generous, willing to share their secrets, fruits of their labor, and their green bounty. I wanted to join in this camaraderie. I wouldn't feel like a real gardener until I too had a steady supply of extra plants to share.

Perhaps I should have steeled myself against the more rampant reproducers, especially in light of the aggressive plants I'd already encountered, but I favor Mirabel Osler's sentiment: "Random seeding can sometimes be a godsend. What gardener doesn't make a mental genuflection on discovering a self-sown group of violas by the doorstep, or on finding a spire of deep blue Jacob's Ladder under the blackish-crimson blooms of rose 'William Lobb'?"

Monitoring the reproductive habits of my shrubs and perennials kept me so busy that I didn't regret ignoring annuals. I sowed a few packets of annual vine seeds, but the only annual plant I actually bought was a mislabeled seedling from the Farmer's Market. The mystery plant bore an unusual and elegant flower in a color exactly suited to my front garden's color scheme; five cream-colored petals wrapped around a wine-red center. It took a detailed reading of two different Thompson and Morgan catalogs before I recognized the plant in a photograph labeled *Hibiscus trionum* 'Simply Love'.

Thompson and Morgan listed it as a half-hardy annual requiring "understanding and care" to grow. I was certain I'd seen the last of it at the end of the Summer. Though I liked it, I didn't want to grow it from seed and plant it out every year. But the next Spring, I happened to notice a seedling with such unusual leaves that I let it grow, curious to see what it would become. It was another 'Simply Love'.

It felt like I'd received a pat on the back from Mother Nature herself. "Okay, Evelyn," she was saying magnanimously, "You've done a fine job with your garden so far. I'll let you keep the *Hibiscus trionum*."

I vowed then that I would continue to give unknown seedlings a season of evaluation, despite the risk of extra work, so I wouldn't miss any other unexpected favors. Mirabel Osler is right. It's a blessing that some plants self-sow, that the garden is always producing new things for its gardener to discover and appreciate.

Not All Loves Last

"I remain baffled; there seems to be no fine line dividing right from wrong as to how to treat a plant. It either takes to you, or it doesn't."

Mirabel Osler, <u>In the Eye of the Garden</u>

My list of possible plants lengthened. Some I wanted for their looks (in a photo, in another garden, in a pot at the nursery) and others for their habits (early-flowering, fruits that attract birds, quick grower). I planted one or two of each, anxious to fit as many different plants into the garden as possible and cautious about committing to any before I sampled many. My friend Christopher taught me this strategy. He calls it "playing the field".

Sadly, caution was justified. Though every new plant enthralled me at first, some infatuations faded on closer acquaintance. Choosing the plants was merely the beginning of our relationship, as a wedding is the beginning of a marriage.

With some plants, one look during the wrong season squashed my enthusiasm. Jacob's ladder (*Polemonium caeruleum*) impressed me at the nursery with its basal rosette of finely divided foliage, so I bought several of the plain green ones and a couple of the variegated (*P. c.* 'Brise d'Anjou'), but then in mid-Summer their promising masses of leaves grew gawky stems topped with disproportionately few tiny blue flowers. I gave them away.

I was excited to find seeds for a double-flowered hollyhock (an *Alcea rosea* cultivar) in the Thompson and Morgan catalog one year. Its pale yellow powderpuffs were a perfect color for my front garden, and the tall stalks would add dramatic accents on either side of the front door. I planted them and, since they're biennial, waited two years for them to bloom. The tight balls of petals looked ungainly. I decided I preferred the curvaceous shape and prominent stamen of the single-flowered hollyhocks. Soon after they bloomed, a strong rainstorm bent their stalks, and with all those heavy flowers, they couldn't right themselves. This made it easier to pull them up.

Extensive reading didn't prevent mistakes. I'd read that evergreens need acidic soil, so I mulched my new yew (*Taxus cuspidata* 'Capitata') with pine needles. The next Spring, when the neighbor's mature yew had light green candles at the tips of its branches, my little yew remained dark green. Worried, I looked up yews in several books and learned that, unlike pines, spruces, and many other evergreens, yews prefer limy soil.

I transferred the pine needles to an azalea, then, feeling like I should be wearing a white lab coat, knelt beside the ailing yew with a chip of limestone rock from my stepping stone path. Using another stone, I scraped limestone dust onto the ground under the yew, buried the limestone fragment among its roots, and watered it copiously. Within a week, it sprouted light green new growth.

Some plants were worth the extra effort it took to find them the right site. The summersweets were like the girl in the old nursery rhyme:

> "There was a little girl who had a little curl
> right in the middle of her forehead.
> When she was good, she was very, very good;
> when she was bad, she was horrid."

They tried my patience to its limit, they were so picky about initial conditions. I planted two full-sized summersweets (*Clethra alnifolia*) side-by-side next to the lilacs. Their soft, sweet fragrance, glossy green leaves, and cheery yellow Fall color persuaded me to plant others, so I added five miniature clethras (*C. a.* 'Hummingbird') under the jack pine. Then one of the full-sized summersweets wasted away, even as the other flourished, and as soon as I planted them, the five small ones began turning brown and dropping their leaves.

According to the books, summersweets need some moisture, some shade, and some acidity. Apparently I had the mix wrong. I moved the small ones to the side yard across the path from the surviving full-sized one, where they didn't like it either. I was about to give up on them, but decided to move them into a recently enlarged bed before buying something else to plant there. They immediately bushed out and flowered later that year. As the soil stayed moist all Summer in that area, though it received only a couple of hours of sunlight per day, I deduced that moisture is more important than sunlight to summersweets.

I couldn't find the right spot for every plant I brought into the garden. I was looking forward to getting to know the Christmas-rose (*Helleborus niger*) and the bronze-leaved cardinal flower (*Lobelia cardinalis* 'Queen Victoria'), but both deserted me during their first Winter. Three elegant white columbines thrived for two years, then abruptly sickened and died. So did three veronicas in another part of the garden.

For three years, my *Euonymus fortunei* 'Green and Gold' bushes arose half-dead every Spring and somehow barely recuperated in time for Winter. As far as I could tell, I'd planted them in the correct soil, moisture, and light conditions. My tendency at first was to hope I was misreading the signs, but after the third year, I admitted failure and gave them to Kristin. Though she lived only a couple of miles from me, her plants regularly leafed out and bloomed one to two weeks ahead of mine. Perhaps the euonymus needed a warmer, more sheltered area, because they sprang to life in her yard and expanded into thick, leafy mounds.

Honestly, I was relieved to see them go. They were daily reminders of how little I knew about how Nature works, even on my own property.

Sometimes, even when research told me a plant wouldn't survive in certain conditions, I planted it there anyway. I guess hope triumphed over common sense. "The side yard won't be too damp for two dozen graceful Dutch iris," I told myself. "That pair of dwarf spruces won't mind receiving only morning sunlight." The plants in question disagreed—the iris drowned and the spruces shaded out—proving the old adage that you might fool yourself but you won't fool Mother Nature.

It was toughest to admit failure with my favorites. The Fireside apple's health nosedived soon after I planted it. The damp, shady side yard kept its roots too wet, and the last branch I'd pruned was black and soft inside. The tree's all-time harvest high was five apples during its second

Summer, but those apples were the best I'd ever tasted—just the right mix of tangy and sweet, and incredibly crisp. I put off doing something until the fourth year, trying to decide whether the tree could be moved or must be removed. The nursery had cautioned against moving it, but I didn't want to lose it to rot, and I couldn't just pull it up and toss it out like I did sickly perennials.

I finally moved it into a new planting bed and decided to give it one more year. If it perked up, I'd add plants around it; if not, I would give up on it. Meanwhile, I was back to figuring out how to block the view between our dining room and the neighbor's kitchen.

Further south in the side yard, the 'President Grevy' lilacs developed chalky white film on their leaves each Summer due to inadequate sunlight and airflow. They weren't dying—many lilacs grow and flower while succumbing to the same fungus—but outbreaks occurred every year. Meanwhile, they started to send suckers up into the gravel path beside them. Some years they didn't flower. These shortcomings confronted me every time I walked down the path or looked out the front porch window. Still, I was reluctant to remove them. After four years they were finally tall enough to block the neighbor's porch windows from our view. So what if they didn't offer much else?

Decisions about whether to keep certain plants became easier after I stumbled across a book called <u>Shrubs and Trees for the Small Place</u> by Peter J. Van Melle. The book was first published in 1943 and was out of print. I found it in a used bookstore that stocked a decent Gardening section. (Used book shopping sprees, I discovered, are exciting treasure hunts; many fabulous garden books have gone out of print and are impossible to find except by chance.)

Van Melle, an opinionated gardener like the rest of us, developed a method for subjectively but scientifically rating shrubs and trees against his list of desirable traits. He gave each plant a numerical score for each of his criteria. The sum of a plant's scores represented its value in the landscape. Plants' final scores could be compared when making decisions.

Since my priorities and opinions differed from Van Melle's, I reworked his criteria into two tiers of characteristics, the most important five being foliage, non-Summer wildlife value, blending ability in the border,

Winter interest, and freedom from serious pests or diseases. I included Autumn interest and early Spring interest as a second tier; they were less important only because those are short seasons here in Minnesota.

I rated the 'President Grevy' lilacs using my criteria. They scored low in the foliage category, though their dark blue-green leaves would be more appealing if they weren't covered in powdery mildew. Their bare legs rose gracefully from skirts of variegated hostas and presented a striking Winter profile of dark branches against the neighbor's gray house. Pruned to attain quick height, they'd taken just two years to raise a seasonal shield between our front porch windows and the neighbor's. They gave birds shelter but no food; as far as I could tell, no animals ate their seeds. They didn't flower reliably, bloom period was short, and they had no striking Spring or Fall leaf color to recommend them.

The lilacs clearly didn't fulfill my expectations for their eight-foot-square planting space, which I had hoped would support some combination of plants—preferably fragrant, preferably evergreen—that could block views, tolerate three hours of filtered sunlight per day, and provide year-round interest. But could any plants meet those expectations?

I scored some of my other shrubs and found that better options already grew in my garden. If I replaced the lilacs with my yew and my surviving full-sized summersweet bush (*Clethra alnifolia* 'Rosea'), the combination would yield year-round interest. The deep green yew foliage would set off the summersweet's bare branches in Winter, lime-green leaves in Spring, pink-white flower spires in Summer, and gold Autumn color. The summersweet's fragrance would waft through the porch windows in Summer, while the yew's subtle, year-round aroma would shyly greet those walking past. Once the yew reached its expected height of eight feet, it would block the view into the neighbor's porch without shutting out sunlight. The summersweet would attain similar height, and unpruned, the two shrubs would fill the area in question. I could prune their lower branches to make room for groundcover plantings.

The lilacs joined the euonymus in Kristin's garden, and I moved the yew and summersweet into their vacated bed. I'd need to wait a few years to regain privacy, but my impatience was receding as my garden filled. My only worry was that the yew preferred lime and the summersweet acid; I hoped I could keep them both happy with occasional applications of pine needles (for the latter) and limestone shavings (for the former).

It's ironic that I decided to give up my own lilacs after feeling so sentimental about the bush our previous landlord cut down. After fostering mine and seeing their failings, I understand his decision to replace the lilacs, though I still cringe at the memory of their violent destruction.

It's also ironic that the tree with which he replaced them was a white birch, which he probably chose for some of the reasons I chose my birches. I can now admire his vision as I imagine that tree bestowing dappled shade and seclusion on the courtyard in Summer and providing the tenants with a spectacular year-round view.

Giving away plants I'd bought and nurtured for four years redoubled my caution about buying new ones. I tried to study the microclimates of my property and to only add plants that had a chance of thriving. Some gardeners will adjust an unsuitable location to fit a preferred plant's needs, but I wanted to find plants that suited each location. My successes and failures taught me that I didn't have total control over the mix of species in my garden. Nature had a voice too, and if I paid close attention, I could sometimes hear it.

Still, I succumbed to occasional infatuations. Like an ex-smoker at the sight of someone lighting up on-screen, I was struck by cravings for plants larger than my garden could accommodate, showy or unusual plants, plants that didn't fit the requirements I'd laid out for each area of my garden. I'd notice a photo, read a description, hear another gardener praising a plant, or meet said plant in a garden or a nursery, and I'd be smitten. I'd long to watch it grow and change through the seasons. I'd mentally search my garden to find a place for it.

If I had allowed myself to buy more roses, my yard would have quickly filled with them. The quintessential impulse plant, they were everywhere—in catalogs and garden centers, florists' shops and grocery stores. Their exquisitely shaped, delicately scented flowers drew me as they have numerous gardeners through the ages.

For years I wanted to plant *Rosa* 'Zephirine Drouhin'—pink flowers, nearly thornless canes, reputedly vigorous even on the north side of a building. I imagined a dozen places to put her, suspecting all the while that, despite the good press, she'd turn out finicky. And I was not a gardener for finicky plants. I wouldn't coddle a rose, give it fertilizer, pick off its dead leaves and throw them in the trash, or dig a trench to bury it every Winter. I was hard pressed to just prune my one 'Golden Wings' rose occasionally.

I adored my rose, though it struggled from the harsh climate and from neglect, dying back to the ground every Fall and sending up a handful of shoots that reached at most four feet during the course of a Summer. 'Golden Wings' blooms are pale creamy yellow when they first open, and gradually they turn to white as if bleached by the sun. The five petals surround a gold and orange ring of stamens. The clove-like smell, strongest on newly opened flowers, is at once old-fashioned and comforting, and just faint enough to entice the sniffer into lingering. It blooms sporadically through the Summer, and after the flowers subside, it produces large, decorative golden hips. I was thrilled that such a treasure survived in my garden, but its murmured complaints—modest growth and bloom—warned me not to subject any of its relatives to such indifference.

Anyway, it is only their flowers that have won roses such disproportionate attention from gardeners and growers. Most people don't regard thorns as a feature, though I like them as a barrier to domestic animals and small children. Many people don't notice hips either, a pity since these can last longer than flowers and occur in a season when decoration is sparser.

On Van Melle's scale and my own, roses score poorly in a landscape like mine, where the soil is rich clay, humidity is high, and Nature packs the plants together. They score higher and look better in desert-style plantings like my mom's and grandma's Idaho gardens, with spaces between plants allowing enough airflow to prevent mildew and keeping down competition for scarce water and nutrients.

Each time I was tempted to buy a rose, I would tell myself these things.

My rose fantasies evolved when I read about another kind of rose, the tough kind that grows in local cemeteries or behind old houses. Robin Chotzinoff devotes a chapter of <u>People With Dirty Hands</u> to such roses—vigorous growers with lifespans of a hundred years or more, well adapted to their local climates. The American Rose Emporium finds and propagates these hardy survivors, selling them on their own roots. Chotzinoff describes the dizzy array of their smells—vanilla, blackberry, peppermint—the delicate single blossoms, and the sheer vigor of the plants, one of which can form a thirty-foot thicket. My pining after 'Zephirine Drouhin' and her ilk dissolved in admiration for their wilder kin, but in a way this was a safer craving, for I knew I couldn't afford the space they needed.

Slowly I learned to choose plants that were suited to my garden, and it was a bittersweet lesson. On the one hand, so many were excluded; on the other, those that got in flourished. Luckily, unrequited desire appeals to my romantic nature, and the losses imposed by limited space and unsuitable conditions lent a not unwelcome poignancy to my garden, a shadow of the road not taken.

Catalog Colonists
(Third Winter)

"With a structure already well planned and established, further plant additions become 'furnishings'; emphasis moves to plants which contribute flowers, fruit, and foliage. The gardener can now concentrate on plants with more fleeting and ephemeral attributes, rather than those of good form and habit which are essential qualities in the initial planning stage."

Penelope Hobhouse, <u>Garden Style</u>

I'll never forget the thrill of reading through my first Thompson and Morgan seed catalog, with its many descriptions and color photos. I could grow any of the plants mentioned for just a few dollars—upside-down trees, sea holly, tropical vines, heirloom vegetables... catalogs expanded the possibilities into infinity.

The only hard part was coping with delayed gratification.

The first Autumn of my garden, I ordered Spring bulbs from the Michigan Bulb Company. Their catalog arrived unsolicited the minute I started gardening. It didn't list plants' Latin names, but at that stage, I didn't care. My order automatically entered me in the company's sweepstakes.

After I planted the crocus, squill, windflowers, and miniature iris, I waited through an interminable Winter. Toward the end of March, when the Winter snowcover melted, I toured the garden every morning before work and every evening on returning. If the weather was clear and the ground dry, I dropped my briefcase on the doorstep and didn't even change my shoes, but paced the edges of the beds, scouring the ground for signs of new life.

A surge of glee hit every time I saw another leaf-tip emerging from the soil, but agony followed while I waited for the small blade to elongate and spread, the stem to rise, the bud to form, and the flower to seductively unfurl. Bulbs are masters of the tease.

As the bulbs bloomed, my first seed order arrived from Thompson and Morgan. I'd ordered in part to thank that company for distributing such a useful compendium, but also to sample a few plants I hadn't seen at the nurseries. The seeds were from bachelor's buttons (*Centaurea montana*) and white musk mallow (*Malva moschata* 'Alba'), both labeled "easy to grow" in the catalog. I sowed them in peat pots in a plastic tray.

The pots looked like circles of thick cardboard. I lined them up in the tray and poured water over them. Each circle grew into a two-inch cylinder of peat enclosed in fine mesh, with a shallow basin on top for planting. I poked two seeds into each moist, spongy basin. Seedlings sprouted within a couple of weeks, and I watered and watched for four more weeks, then planted them, pots and all, out in the garden. This way of transplanting (in the peat pot) keeps the fragile seedlings' root systems intact and minimizes their shock on being introduced to their new environments.

The bachelor's buttons, some of the earliest perennials to leaf or bloom in my garden, unfurled velvety gray-green leaves in early Spring when the only other signs of life were bulbs and rock cress. Their green buds are cross-hatched like pineapples. Tufts of blue petals sprout from their tips and open into wispy blue-purple flowers that seem to recede, enticing you to lean closer.

The musk mallows wear lacy leaves on loosely arranged, floppy stems. Their flowers are pale gray-white, two inches across, with shell pink centers. They bloom sporadically all Summer even in part-shade.

Though I chose both species for their ready germination, I was surprised by how eagerly they self-sowed in the mulched beds. I could have scattered their seeds directly and saved the effort of peat pots for more reluctant flowers. Their annual crops of seedlings would create work for me, and I would have to decide if their presence was worth that work.

During our second Winter in the new house, I bought my first mail-order plants. I'd spent two years in a frenzy of planting, so the delay between buying and receiving no longer seemed unbearable. Instead it sounded like a fine trade-off for cheaper (though smaller) plants, volume discounts, and greater variety.

The garden club met in December to share favorite catalogs, and I phoned many of their toll-free numbers to request my own copies. I also requested catalogs from several nurseries listed in Taylor's Guide to Specialty Nurseries. Catalogs started arriving several days after my first phone call, and by early February I had a pile of thirty or forty. I spent the evenings sitting in front of the fire and reading them straight through, dogearing pages and circling the plants that intrigued me.

Though I circled annuals, vegetables, and perennials, with supreme effort I restricted my first orders to groundcovers and filler plants for which I could find a permanent place in the front or side beds. I was anxious to clothe these areas with plants so they would feel more finished and resist weeds.

I also curbed my ordering because shipping dates were uncertain. Whereas seed packets can be shipped within days of placing an order, live plants can only travel during the window between too-cold weather and too-hot weather. The fine print in the catalogs said my preferred arrival date could only be met approximately, yet it cautioned that plants should be unwrapped and watered as soon as they arrived, and planted within a day or two if possible. I concluded that I would need to stay home between mid-May and mid-June, ready to receive my plants whenever each nursery decided to ship them.

George and I had planned a vacation during the last two weeks of May. I figured I'd need two weeks to settle in the new plants before we abandoned them, so although our average last frost date is May 15, I requested delivery on May 1 and crossed my fingers.

I placed the first order with Bluestone Perennials of Ohio. Their catalog provided color photos and information to help gardeners find the right plant for a certain place. Each entry included the Latin name and cold-hardiness zone of the plant, charts for bloom period and shade tolerance, and symbols marking the plants that favor southern or northern climates, moist or dry soil, much or little care. Bluestone offered especially competitive prices on groundcovers, sold in lots of six, and a "buy 2, get 1 free" special for those who ordered by March. But the clincher was a fellow garden club member's recommendation. "I've ordered from Bluestone for years," she assured me. "The plants are always healthy and arrive right on schedule."

I placed my other order with an independent grower from Georgia who was listed in Taylor's Guide to Specialty Nurseries. He sold hard-to-find woodland species at prices that beat any others I'd seen. His catalog was a photocopied sheaf of typed pages that spared one line per plant, giving its Latin name, cold-hardiness zone, and a brief physical description. In addition to plants, he offered over eighty horticulture and botany books, some at discount prices.

The plants from Bluestone Perennials arrived April 30, a day before the target date. The ground was thawed enough for planting. The plants were healthy and green, and in fact had outgrown their four-inch pots by the time they reached me.

The largest were sweet woodruff (*Galium odorata* or *Asperula odorata*), a groundcover for damp, low-light areas. Nearly every source of this plant mentioned that it was once used to make May wine, though none explained what May wine was. Richter's Herb Catalog, from a Canadian specialist nursery, gave more information than most with its cryptic description: "traditional German punch". As I planted the sweet woodruff, I found myself wondering if anyone still makes May wine, and why sellers would choose a non-visual bit of trivia to describe such a visually inviting plant. Circular tiers of lance-shaped leaves radiate from each upright stem, creating a six-inch-high mat of identical green pillars. In mid-May, white flowers emerge like stars atop tiny Christmas trees.

I planted sweet woodruff in the damp side yard, where its fresh green foliage obligingly spread unhindered by excess acid, lime, or shade. It swept under the azaleas, covering the layer of pine needle mulch; it paraded across the limestone stepping stones unconcerned by alkalinity; and it even hung on under the hostas, where sunlight did not penetrate. I had read that sweet woodruff could be aggressive, but it seemed easy enough to pull out unwanted sections; the plant crept openly across the surface, resorting to neither the devious burrowing of creeping Charlie nor the wanton seed-scattering of the ladybells.

My order also included a dozen plants of *Campanula carpatica*, which, despite its possible relation to the ladybells, proved an uncommonly slow grower. After several years my plants remained grapefruit-sized clumps of toothed leaves covered in Summer with blue ('Blue Clips') or white ('White Clips') upturned tulip-shaped flowers. Though I tried mixing some with taller perennials, these campanulas were quickly submerged by other plants' foliage. They grow (and look) best on a sunny slope among rocks and shorter groundcovers.

The half-dozen mother-of-thyme (*Thymus serpyllum*) plants quickly repaid my investment. Within a couple of years, each expanded into a flat cushion two feet across, despite my taking numerous divisions from their edges with a trowel. I distributed the divisions around the edges of the sunny front beds, and they crept out onto the warm cement walk. In early Summer, their dense mats of tiny round leaves poke up fingers of pink bloom. Brushing past them releases a spicy aroma from their crushed leaves.

I also planted a couple of pieces in a sunny section of the gravel path, scooping away the gravel and setting a plant in the hollow, then mounding its roots with a handful of soil before covering it again with the gravel. Since the quick drainage leaves them vulnerable to drying out, these gravel-bedded individuals needed more water during their first year than those in the wood-chip-mulched planting beds, but I stopped supplemental watering in their second year with no ill effects. Light foot traffic doesn't harm them, and they turn deep purple in Winter while their planting-bed cousins stay green under a blanket of leaves, then snow.

The final groundcover from my Bluestone order was a white-flowered deadnettle (*Lamium maculatum* 'White Nancy'). Its leaves, silvery white mottled with light green, brighten the dark northeast corner of the house, where three tiny plants managed to clothe a square yard of ground within a year. Full shade doesn't diminish the deadnettle's vigor. It covers lean soil densely, shading out most new seedlings and successfully defending its territory against creeping Charlie. However, it seems content to mingle politely with sweet woodruff, whose bright green pillars jut up at intervals through its ghostly blanket.

Gambling on unprecedented patience, my order also included three baby yews (*Taxus cuspidata* 'Capitata'). Each bush was a six-inch stem with two short branches. Years would pass before they were large enough to be noticeable in a border. I planted them where I hoped their twelve-foot-tall final forms would fit into my still-unfinished design for the backyard, then I tried to focus on their good qualities and not how slowly they grow.

Ten days elapsed after my plants arrived from Bluestone, and each day I expected to see the shipment from the other nursery. When I finally phoned the owner to ask about the delay, he apologized that my delivery date must have confounded the shippers, who'd filled local orders months before. He assured me that my plants would arrive as soon as possible.

We returned from a weekend trip to find a desolate box on the doorstep. Inside lay the dried-up stems of two dozen wintergreens and a dozen Solomon's seals, along with the still-green foliage of a dozen miniature hostas. I tried to coax the plants back to health by watering them profusely, planting them, then watering them again.

The hostas, bless their stubborn green souls, sprang back to life. I had ordered a mix of unlabeled varieties, which appealed both for the price discount and for the challenge of discovering their identities. Their foliage displayed admirable variety—yellow, green, blue, and two-toned. Several of the specimens spread by runners, while others formed clumps. I planted them in a row along the back sidewalk until I could decide where to put them permanently.

The other plants recuperated more slowly from their traumatic journey. *Gaultheria procumbens*, one of several species used to derive wintergreen flavoring, caught my fancy when my friend Peter served me wintergreen tea one evening years before.

"I collected these leaves myself." He took a clay jar from his cupboard, opened the lid, and held the jar out. As I inhaled the sharp, well-named fragrance, he muttered, "That must have been thirty years ago. These leaves are older than you are." Despite their age, they made delicious tea and a precious memory.

Looking at the sparse plantlets before me, I wondered how many years they would need to generate enough leaves for one pot of tea. Each plant was a wiry horizontal stem with a couple of vertical branches. A few shiny leaves, dark olive-green, grew from the tips of each branch. I saw no white bell-shaped flowers or red berries from them that Summer, but their leaves did turn a deep purple in Autumn. Sadly, the next Spring only half the wintergreens reappeared.

The Solomon's seal (*Polygonatum biflorum*) fared worse. These ephemeral woodland natives send up two-foot arching stems from which droplets of white bellflowers hang. They grow in several Minnesota state parks, and I always feel lucky to catch them during their short window of aboveground display.

I planted six under the jack pine in front and the other six under a pagoda dogwood in back to give them a range of soil acidity and moisture. They gradually sank into the soil and refused to come out again.

I took these failures hard and decided to limit my future mail-orders to northern nurseries, since the plants' origin in Georgia probably dictated their doom in my Saint Paul garden. This strategy has increased the survival rate of my purchases.

Though every unknown nursery is a gamble, and though I've found only a few mail-order sources that delight me with every order, the lower cost and wider variety of the plants keep me hungry for catalogs. Browsing them remains an essential element in my repertoire of Winter pleasures.

More and Fewer

*"It is one of the inevitable and unfortunate correlations of gardening that
the more the gardener loves plants, the more difficult it becomes to achieve
the quality of repose."*

Joe Eck, <u>Elements of Garden Design</u>

Where our narrow path through the side yard widened and began
a stately curve around the back of the house, I planted five amur maples
(*Acer ginnala*) spaced five feet apart. Just over the fence from my new
Maple Grove was the neighbor's bustling back entrance, a vantage point
from which our entire backyard was visible.

I was reading Julie Messervy's <u>The Inward Garden</u> at the time.
Messervy explains that certain iconic landscapes—island, valley, grove—
provoke emotional responses in us. "One secret to becoming a good designer," she writes, "Is to acquire a wide-ranging and expanding repertoire
of images that resonate both within yourself and in others."

For me, a grove represents privacy and serenity, neither of which
existed in our backyard. I hoped that my trees would soften other noise
with their rustling and that their leafy canopy would hide most of our
backyard from view. If they didn't perform these functions as well as I'd
anticipated, perhaps the symbolic qualities of the grove would soothe me.

At first I envisioned a grove of Japanese maples (*Acer palmatum*),
but they can die down to the snow level during harsh Winters in zone 4.
Amur maples are a good substitute in northern climates. They grow ten
to fifteen feet high and provide year-round interest. Their leaves, though
not as lacy as those of some Japanese maples, are long-lobed and turn fiery
orange-red in Autumn, and their seedpods emerge red-tinted in Spring,
turn green and finally gold, then hang on their branches all Winter. They
also self-sow copiously and invade remnant and restored prairies in my
region of the U.S., but I wouldn't learn that for years after planting my

trees.

I planned to trim the maples high to form a ceiling suspended on bare trunks. Eventually the arborvitae that I'd planted along the property line would rise in a feathery, evergreen wall behind them.

Under the maples, I distributed a dozen red-leaved heucheras (*H. micrantha* var. *diversifolia* 'Palace Purple') from the Farmer's Market. Each had only a few small leaves, and they browned without daily watering during the first two weeks, but within a couple of months they grew into mounds a foot across with five-inch leaves that flushed deep red and crinkled around the edges. In late Summer they hoisted tall wiry stalks carrying sprays of shell-pink flowers that lit up against their dark leaves.

It's not always the case that a plant's flowers complement its foliage so well—witness the jolt of mauve flowers among the chartreuse leaves of *Spiraea japonica* 'Goldmound', or the disproportionate heads of double blooms exploding above the dignified foliage of a peony.

Among the heucheras, I scattered a package of forget-me-not seeds, which surprised me by sprouting in masses a few weeks afterward, their blooms wafting like blue clouds above their tidy foliage. I'd seen these clouds hovering on the forest floors of northern Wisconsin, their pale haze of flowers electric in some lights and barely visible in others. My seeds were from *Myosotis sylvatica* 'Blue Bird', which isn't one of the native *Myosotis*, but to my delight, the blue haze that appeared in my garden was the same one I'd seen in the woods.

During the rest of the Summer, I added other plants to the Maple Grove, varieties that I hoped would appreciate the damp, limy partial shade: a red creeping sedum, a red sempervivum, a Culver's root (*Veronicastrum virginicum*), a couple of variegated Jacob's ladders, a ground dogwood (*Cornus canadensis*), and astilbes with pink and white plumes (*A. chinensis*).

In the Fall I planted a dozen Chinese tulips (*Tulipa acuminata*), which I'd never seen but came across in the Daffodil Mart catalog. They're not like any other flower that I know. Their petals are wide and yellow at the base, narrowing to vertical red tendrils at the tops. With their flame-like shapes and warm coloring, and their nearly leafless eighteen-inch stems, they look like miniature torches held aloft.

While these tulips were flowering, the forget-me-nots bloomed again. I crouched down in the path to admire them and frowned. Too many other plants disrupted the blue haze, elbowing each other, shouting for attention. As an obsessed gardener, I should have doted on all my plants, but my stubborn eyes wanted only to erase the others and sink into the soothing blueness of the forget-me-nots.

I re-examined my mental picture of an ideal grove. Stark tree trunks towered over a muted blanket of plants. The air was still, the mood serene, inviting the mind to wander. When the picture and the feel of the place were clear, I gritted my teeth and redesigned the Maple Grove to more closely resemble this vision.

Noel Kingsbury helped me. In The New Perennial Garden, he discusses how to create a natural-looking, interesting community of plants. He suggests learning plants' growth habits. Some plants are architectural and do better as isolated specimens, he says, and these should be placed first. Others need to be planted in drifts to have enough visual impact, and they should be set in place next. Finally, in all areas except dense shade, it's important to clothe the ground with matrix plants, locally abundant species that fill in among the more prominent plants and give a landscape continuity.

I'd already discovered that how plants reproduce affects how well they mingle. Kingsbury convinced me that knowing plants' growth habits is another key to designing healthy, stable communities.

For the past year, I had observed my Maple Grove denizens. I'd seen that the forget-me-nots are a fluid and social species. Each plant lives only a year or two, but casts gobs of seed, and in damp areas like my side garden, seedlings come up thick, ready to replace their parents. Individual plants' low rosettes of leaves mesh into a seamless carpet, while above them the flowers float like airy clouds. Their cool, pale coloring makes it easy to scan them without pausing to focus your eyes. They would make an ideal matrix plant for the grove. I scattered more seed to help them spread.

The red-leaved heucheras are more striking as individuals. Given a few years, each forms a two- to three-foot mound with long flower spikes rising from the center. Each of them wants only to build a larger clump of larger leaves every year. Not only does their shape demand attention, so does their color, a deep maroon-purple. Where I planted several together, they made a visual roller coaster when they flowered: my eyes were drawn across leaves, up flower spikes, then down across more leaves. Too many of these down-up-downs were visually exhausting. I decided that the heucheras should be the occasional boulders around which my river of forget-me-nots flowed.

The flame-flowered tulips thrust up a single stem and one flower; they must be grouped to have any visual impact, but planting them too thickly would obscure their dramatic individual forms and leave a noticeable gap after their short bloom period. I'd keep the dozen, which were planted two and three to a hole, for a mid-Spring accent.

Those four species formed my new plant community for the Maple Grove: maples, heucheras, forget-me-nots, and tulips. The new planting scheme would produce an orderly procession of interesting scenes throughout the year. It meant I must move or give away all the other plants that had taken up residence there. I had to summon all my willpower to carry it out.

In the end, I couldn't quite do it. It felt too dull and predictable. Then I remembered an old quilt-making tradition. The seamstress deviates once from the pattern to mark the quilt as handmade. For instance, in a checkerboard pattern of red and black, she might substitute a blue square for one of the black ones.

In the same spirit, I decided to allow one deviation from the pattern I'd designed, and so under one of the maples I kept a trio of wild geraniums (whose precise name I don't know, as they came from a friend's garden) with shocking magenta flowers. Their growth habit wasn't arresting enough to disrupt the grand pattern; they crawled among the other plants, throwing up leaves and flowers at intervals. To the restrained character of the grove they added whimsy, and a reminder not to take gardening so seriously.

The Gardener's Sanity
(Third Summer)

"Sometimes a place apart, one that asks little and does not confront the roving, anxious eye with the chores of deadheading, raking, pruning, tying in, tying up, cutting back, dividing, replanting... is necessary to the gardener's sanity and even to the garden's continued existence."

Joe Eck, Elements of Garden Design

The front garden presented a lively view from the three-season porch. Herbs and yellow flowers crowded the sunny beds, the Woody Border was thick with fruiting and berrying shrubs, and the Butterfly Garden hosted all manner of flitting, buzzing insects. Birds feasted year-round and splashed in the baths.

From this bustling place, the stepping-stone path led around the house and through a narrow, hidden garden where yellows were absent and foliage—vines and evergreens—cloaked the high trellis walls. Pink and white accents lightened the greens and made the winding path seem enchanted, ethereal.

When the path entered the Maple Grove, the colors deepened to wine-red, blue, and glaucous green. The maples spread a thick ceiling of leaves above the shaggy evergreen wall of arborvitae. The greens and blues radiated calm, and the reds focused attention within the grove. Every Fall, the ceiling turned a festive crimson.

The back yard kept the relaxed mood but felt spacious rather than enclosed. The ceiling gave way to sky. The path widened and branched, leading to a patio and a pond. Blue and gray foliage pleasantly blurred together and receded from view, drawing thoughts and attention away, encouraging the eyes to rest while it tantalized the other senses. Grasses and textured leaves rustled in the slightest breeze. Aromatic herbs and ev-

ergreens exuded savory scents. Trees and shaded rocks captured cool air
in Summer and warm air in Spring and Fall, and flowers were rare, which
discouraged pesky bugs.

Best of all, the back yard contained a private space in which a
person could read or think without interruption. Noises from outside did
intrude—children shrieking, hounds baying, motorcycles, lawnmowers,
car engines, and distant sirens—but at times, even in that urban neighborhood, the sounds miraculously ceased, and peace reigned. And on Summer
evenings, when people swarmed outdoors to play radios and grill things,
the calming masses of foliage, the peaceful blues and silvers, the sounds of
grass shivering in the wind, and the smells of sage and spruce tempered
the bustling environment.

This, at least, was my fantasy about what my garden could become
with a little old-fashioned toil and sweat. I hadn't realized it would take so
long. By the third Summer, the garden was still far from my ideal: front
Woody Border too sparse, vines recalcitrant, backyard just a weedy lawn.

I was seeing some progress. Clumps of blackeyed Susans and sweet
woodruff and thyme were spreading. Shrubs and trees, though not yet providing the privacy and interest I imagined, still showed noticeable growth
every year.

However, my expectations kept rising. Over the years, my garden
dreams became more lavish and more detailed. Their vividness spurred
me to keep working, to narrow the gap between real garden and dream
garden.

It seemed like I was always thinking about the garden. On the rare
occasions that I tried to sit and rest outdoors, my eyes darted around, scan-
ning for imperfections, while I reflexively made lists of chores and projects
in my head and worked out what plants or structures should go where.

I'd built a garden that engaged my interest and energy, but I
needed a place outdoors where I could regenerate—a haven not only from
neighborhood sounds, sights, and smells, but also from the demands of
the garden. In my plan, this haven was a roughly sixteen-foot-square area
in the center of the backyard; it would have a place to sit and perhaps,
someday, a pond. Aside from a rock patio behind the house, paths, and
the parking area, the rest of the backyard would be a sort of buffer zone,

thickly planted to provide as much serenity and privacy as possible for the area they enclosed.

I began work on the backyard during our third Summer in the house. First I smothered the three areas that would become the planted buffer zone.

One of these areas, located between the future Haven and the future rock patio, enlarged a small vegetable patch from the previous two Summers. I made a typical new-gardener blunder and planted sixteen tomato plants the first year. I germinated two dozen tomato seedlings in little peat pots, and they grew rapidly, fueling my confidence. They were yellow pear tomatoes—small enough to pop into your mouth whole, picturesque split open on a salad, and unavailable in grocery stores or the Farmer's Market. I suspected I might have grown too many seedlings, but after rearing them, I couldn't kill them. I pawned nine of them off on my co-workers, then our friend Val offered me a sixteenth plant, an heirloom plum tomato his family had brought from Italy, from which he had been collecting and saving seeds for years. It was an offer I couldn't refuse.

The tomato plants grew like weeds, and I, busy with long-term things like shrubs and paths, couldn't be bothered to stake them up. Suddenly it was too late. They were a tangle of sinuous stems, dragging each other earthward, transforming my vegetable garden into a giant tomato thicket under which all else was smothered. We ate a lot of tomatoes that Summer, but many fell to the ground and rotted before the first frost, when I yanked up the whole sorry mess and dragged it to the compost heap.

The following Summer, feeling wiser about the ways of vegetables, I ruthlessly pulled or gave away all but four of the seedlings that grew up from the old tomato patch. Even these four proved too many. As the Summer progressed, they toppled their flimsy metal cages with stems that were ten feet long and weighted down with fruit. I resolved not to grow tomatoes again until I built large wooden frames like Val's.

The twice-used and currently dormant vegetable bed bordered one edge of my planned Haven, and since no plants would scream high-maintenance like vegetables did, I faced a pivotal choice. In the Maple Grove, I'd cut down on variety to achieve serenity, but should I—could I—give up fresh pear tomatoes as well?

An inner voice said that I wouldn't be able to relax within sight of the vegetables, and another stubbornly pointed out that we couldn't buy pear tomatoes in the store, and furthermore I would likely not encounter the other enticing vegetables from the catalogs unless I grew them myself: multi-colored hot peppers from one bush, loofah gourds, eggplants shaped like tiny pumpkins… I let the voices argue, refusing to yield to either one, while I enlarged the bed and covered it with mulch and newspapers. It would lie unplanted until I could decide.

The second buffer zone extended along the west edge of the Haven, between it and a walkway connecting the house to the garage. The area was lightly shaded by a black locust (*Robinia pseudoacacia*) tree. I planted a baby Black Hills spruce (*Picea glauca* var. *densata*) at the northwest corner of the bed; it would grow to block the prevailing winter winds and per-haps extend the season of use for the Haven. It might not happen during my tenure in the house, but I tried not to let that discourage me. Near the spruce, I planted a couple of dwarf highbush cranberries (*Viburnum trilobum* 'Bailey's Compact'), medium-sized shrubs with dense, graceful foliage.

The third bed ran along the south wall of the garage at the back edge of the property. Though it was only four feet wide, this planting area would at least visually separate the Haven from the garage wall.

The south wall of a building is a great spot for growing plants that aren't hardy elsewhere in the garden, especially if there is additional shel-ter along one or both sides of the planting area. As it was such a prime location, I happily nursed fantasies of espaliered Asian pear trees, jasmine vines, and the Zone 6-hardy figs I'd encountered in a catalog of fruits for home gardens. But as with the vegetable bed, I was reluctant to decide without mulling over my options first, so I covered the third bed with newspapers and mulch and left it unplanted too. By the next Summer, the dormant beds would generate a layer of rich, weed-free topsoil, and mean-while, I would dream of figs.

Our Garden Rocks

"Stone is evocative. It can carry you away to craggy peaks of distant mountains, take you close to the bones of the earth, or hint at the presence of a meandering brook or bubbling spring."

Barbara Pleasant, <u>Garden Stone</u>

The search for cheap limestone led me to a landscape supply yard located forty minutes from my house (but worth the drive due to the lower prices). Often, when I had a few free hours, I borrowed George's truck and drove out to this dusty lot. In the space of two football fields, piles of gravel, sand, and mulch hulked on the bare ground among stacks of paving stone and groups of boulders.

Most of the customers were builders who placed their orders over the phone, then sent a truck to pick up the goods. A customer on foot in the lot was a rare sight, but I enjoyed wandering between the trucks like a child among benevolent dinosaurs. I examined the different types of rock, squeezing my eyes shut and holding my breath each time a truck rumbled past and sent up a vicious tornado of dust.

Eventually, an employee would notice me and drive over in one of the smaller tractors to answer my questions and help calculate how much of each material I needed. When I was ready to load, I drove George's truck into the lot, and soon a helpful tractor would chug over to load the materials I'd chosen.

Rocks were priced per ton and loose materials by cubic yard (or yard, for short). Sometimes I wanted a yard of mulch, sometimes half a yard of pea gravel, and usually I topped the load with irregular slabs of Minnesota Yellow limestone. I avoided the thinnest slabs and chose those that were three to four inches thick but not too heavy for me to carry: one-person rocks. I used them for the stepping stone path alongside the house and for working paths that wandered through my planting beds. I planned to build the patios from the same stones, though I was sorely tempted by the Colorado sandstone that lay stacked at the back of the lot.

The Colorado sandstone was the object of one of my more potent garden fantasies. The irregular slabs were larger and thinner than my limestone pieces, still one-person rocks, but barely. Their grainy texture recalled the desert, but their color—exotic orange embellished with dark red tiger stripes—spoke of the jungle.

I imagined standing on a patio made of those stones, with orange Turk's-cap lilies growing on one side of me, and on the other, trellis walls overhung with native vines—orange-flowered trumpet vine (*Campsis radicans*) and bright-berried bittersweet (*Celastrus scandens*). I could hear the distant hiss and growl of fierce jungle cats, the cool swish of thigh-thick snakes. I could feel sweat dripping, feel my footsteps thudding on soft, dry dirt. The image was so vivid I nearly succumbed to it on several occasions, but I could only find one place for the sandstone in my garden, and I couldn't subvert my blue and gray Haven with those intense orange rocks.

After several trips to buy landscaping materials, I started taking a plastic tarp so I could carry two loads, say half a yard of limestone sand and half a yard of wood chip mulch, without mixing them. After the first load was dumped into the truck bed, I'd vault up and spread the tarp across that load, and when I was safely out of the way, the tractor would dump a second load on the tarp.

Choosing the materials was fun, but the hard work began when I returned home to unload them. In five seconds, the giant shovel emptied half a yard of pea gravel into the truck. Given several hours, I could shovel that gravel into my wheelbarrow, wheel it into the garden, dump it, and return for more until, like the slow drip of water wearing a basin into stone, by diligent repetition I emptied the truck.

One afternoon during the third Summer of my garden, I wandered into the supply yard and stopped in awe. Then I dragged my friend Margaret toward the three magnificent specimens of Minnesota Yellow limestone that lounged near the pile of stepping stones. The new arrivals were table-top-sized, roughly round, five feet across, and four to five inches thick. They were definitely not one-person rocks. They half-stood and half-reclined on the gravel, daring me to take them.

I drew closer to examine their gritty, pocked surfaces. Lightly I skimmed a fingertip across a brittle white crust of lichen. I wanted these rocks—their age, their size, and their character—for my garden.

To some people rocks are decorative, to others annoying. To me they symbolize timelessness, invulnerability, and wisdom. The larger ones carry a particular sense of the ancient. It fascinates me how rocks crumble slowly into soil, how they collect lichens and moss, how they rise to the surface of the fields each year on my grandparents' farm in southern Idaho.

I inherited my love of rocks from my grandma, who wrestled lava boulders from those fields and piled them in circles to create terraced rock gardens that she filled with bright annuals—moss rose, marigolds, petunias, dusty millers. She built her own version of the weather-sculpted canyon walls and buttes that occur naturally in the surrounding landscape.

I decided to follow her example and build a rock structure that would echo Minnesota's exposed rocky stretches—the limestone bluffs along the Mississippi River and the bare bedrock that surfaces in parts of northern Minnesota. My front patio would suggest an outcrop of stone, scraped clean by wind or glacier, cracked and eroded by the elements.

My plans for finishing the backyard Haven that Summer blew away like topsoil from a freshly plowed field. I bought two of the tabletop rocks that day to prevent their being sold off. Then I went home and paced around the front yard, thinking feverishly about how I would get them to their new location, the grassy oblong in front of the house.

The problem was that I had already planted the areas around the proposed front patio. No space remained across which a soil-compacting tractor could haul my new rocks to their destination. Well, our neighbor's open swath of lawn offered a path, but even tough turf would suffer when crushed by a tractor bearing a five-hundred-pound rock, and after the pergola mishap, I didn't want to inconvenience them with another of my landscaping projects. I had to find another way.

"Why don't you use a piano dolly?" suggested my brilliant husband George. I'd never seen one, but it sounded sturdy enough to wheel the new rocks from the backyard, via sidewalks, straight to the edge of the proposed patio. That is, if I could find a way to stand the rocks up and maneuver them onto the dolly.

It sounded easier than hauling the rocks up the front slope which, except for a skinny flight of steps, was encrusted with shrubs. I phoned the landscape company and told them to deliver the rocks to the back. Then I arranged the labor, calling upon George, who said he'd help with garden projects I couldn't do alone; our neighbor Jeff, whose imagination was piqued by the idea of having an Exposed Bedrock Patio next door; and our friend Kurt, who was the only attendant at our wedding and so feels a certain familial obligation toward us.

The day the rocks were to be delivered, I spent the afternoon digging a bed approximately ten feet by six in area and eight inches deep. I used the excavated dirt and sod to build one mound at the edge of the Butterfly Garden and another in one of the fallow back beds. The mounds would make effective sound barriers, break up the too-flat feel of the garden, and look lovely planted with creeping plants and bulbs. It beat paying someone to haul away good soil.

While I was taking a break from digging, a dump truck arrived. It carried the two giant rocks comfortably supported on a couple of cubic yards of sand, which kept them from cracking during transit and would form the subsurface of the new patio.

I showed the driver the tarp I'd spread in the backyard. He explained that he'd back up to it and tilt the truck bed slowly so the sand would slide out first, cushioning the rocks' fall. I stood back, leaning on my shovel, to watch the process. The front edge of the truck bed rose slowly. Nothing happened until it was tilted at a forty-five degree angle, then all at once the rocks and sand shot onto the tarp. The sheepish driver accepted my check without comment and sped away while I was still laughing.

The rocks weren't hurt. The only damage was the two large holes they ripped in my tarp as they landed. The tarp caught most of the sand, which I spread a couple of inches deep across my fresh excavation. The remainder would fill spaces between the rocks once they were laid.

My three fearless workers arrived a couple of hours before dusk. I was horrified to realize that I had been so engrossed in digging, mound-building, and sand-spreading that I'd forgotten to find a piano dolly.

They were good sports about this lapse. After a few minutes of creative discussion, we decided to tie some of the hemp rope left over from the pergola around one rock, ratchet it onto a boat trailer, tow it around the block to the front of the house, back it up over the curb and onto the sidewalk, unhitch the trailer from the truck, tie another rope around the jack pine and use it to leverage the rock and trailer up the neighbor's grassy slope, push said rock and trailer across their lawn to the edge of the patio bed, and lift one end of the trailer to slide the rock into the sand.

Plan B worked on the first rock, but when we tried it with the second, the trailer jackknifed as it was backing over the curb. The tongue of the trailer bent nearly ninety degrees and was rendered useless. Only by brute force did we manage to haul the rock and broken trailer over the curb, up the slope, and to the edge of the patio, then slide the rock onto the ground near its sister. By this time four or five neighbors had happened onto our project and pitched in.

When the second rock slid into place, a collective sigh rose up from all, punctuated by a few snide remarks and shakes of the head that were quelled when I invited everyone to have a drink on me at a nearby watering hole.

The Exposed Bedrock Patio looked permanent right away, and it would only improve as plants crept across the gaps between rocks. The next day I watched the rain puddle on its shallow-cratered surfaces and wished I'd bought the third rock too, but I couldn't think of anyone I could sucker into helping me move it.

Nearly everyone we knew soon heard the story of the rocks. Each time the tale was told, the rocks grew larger, the dangers greater, and my desire for them more inconceivable. No doubt years from now the Day the Rocks Were Moved will be a local legend, and whoever lives in the house can charge tourists to view them, because I doubt they will be moved again.

Vermin Are Wildlife Too

*"When I started gardening, I had no idea that I would get so intimate
with the lives of bugs."*

Amy Stewart, <u>From the Ground Up</u>

Perhaps I should reconsider my harsh judgment of double-flowered peonies. I loved their huge blooms until I discovered that they harbored vermin. When I was twelve, I gathered a bouquet of pink ones (every garden seems to have some) and set them in a vase on the dining table, onto which ants rapidly dropped like a horde of skydivers. Halfway through setting the table for lunch, I finally noticed the ants and, aghast at the flowers' betrayal, I hustled them out the door and out of my good opinion forever.

I'm not saying I don't appreciate ants—they fascinate me when observed in their natural habitats. Like the roly-poly bugs I found in the Seattle sidewalks and the grasshoppers that sunbathed on the lichen-spotted rock walls of my grandparents' cellar, they are only labeled vermin indoors. Outside they are just insects, a group more unique and varied than larger garden denizens, with the possible exception of gardeners.

Making a garden introduced me to new insects. Every element that I added seemed to invite its own associated bugs. One afternoon I found swarming around the cheery gold blooms of *Heliopsis helianthoides* subsp. *scabra* 'Summer Sun' a cluster of insects that looked like green bees. The bees didn't appear to be interested in any of the other plants in the yard, and the next year, when the 'Summer Suns' were accidentally pulled in a too-hasty weeding spree, their insect pals did not return either.

A batch of white aphids appeared on the honeysuckle, clustered so thickly around the stems that I thought they were mildew. I was reaching out to rub a stem clean when I noticed the mildew roiling and snatched my hand away again. If I peered into the morass, I could see individual bodies; they wriggled across the plant and each other, oblivious to all but their hunger for plant sap. Later in the Summer, a swarm of pale yellow aphids replaced them, and the next Spring it was whites again.

A dramatic pink-flowered swamp milkweed (*Asclepias incarnata*) grew up in the driveway, seeded by a backyard prairie down the alley. When I examined it closely, its orange stems turned out to be green beneath their coat of orange aphids.

One day I was admiring a forsythia's dark blue-green foliage, noting how the leaves were the opposite of glossy, so non-reflective that they receded from view, unlike the eye-catching shiny leaves of the nearby flowering quince. The forsythia foliage shut out light from its innermost branches. I wondered if its density appealed to nesting birds. As I peered into a gloomy recess, my eyes fixed on an inch-long black creature perched on a leaf in the shadows. Its front end resembled a dragonfly, but its posterior curled back on itself like a scorpion's tail. I jerked my exposed face away.

Dragonflies and damselflies appeared when I set up a birdbath in the front yard. Some were dark brown, some bright turquoise blue, and others the intense red of cardinals. They were live decorations, hovering and darting.

After I covered the back lawn with gravel and mulched beds, a cricket moved in. Occasionally I'd spot it walking over the small rocks, and its chirping accompanied my labors. I wished others would join it, but it was either an outcast or a pioneer.

Many kinds of bees visited our garden, and with Farrand's <u>Insects and Spiders</u>, I identified honeybees, bumblebees, paper wasps, yellow jackets, and mud daubers. The last three groups fell away when I removed the stacks of rotted firewood from the backyard, and I'm afraid I didn't miss them. My favorites are the big furry queen bumblebees, whose rumbling presence is at once industrious and comforting. They remind me of my mom, Deborah, whose name means "busy bee" and who also displays those two qualities.

The aforementioned <u>Insects and Spiders</u> didn't help me to identify the terrifying black bug or the green bees or the multicolored aphids, and it gave the merest description of those animals that it did include. If I hadn't read <u>Noah's Garden</u>, I would not have identified my orange aphids as such, but Sara Stein writes about the same orange aphids appearing on her swamp milkweed.

Curiosity led me to browse the bookstores for a more comprehensive reference on insects, one with habitat information and glossy color photos to help a novice like me learn all about my backyard bugs. I found no such reference. Maybe it's out there still waiting to be discovered during my next foray into the bookstore, or maybe home gardeners have not yet expressed a clear interest in this information.

There exists, on the other hand, an extraordinary reference to fungi. While browsing in a used bookstore, I stumbled upon Polese and Lamaison's <u>The Great Encyclopedia of Mushrooms</u>. It separates mushrooms into nine groups that share key characteristics. Each species is described and pictured in full color, with its Latin name, edibility, average size, similar species, where it is commonly found, and an extremely detailed physical description including age- and area-related variations. Unfortunately, I am overly timid about handling mushrooms, so I've only been able to successfully identify the unusual ones.

One day under the white birch, I discovered a small cup an inch or two wide with tiny white balls inside. I called a neighbor over, and we speculated that it could be eggs, maybe those of a frog or newt. I offered her one of the tiny nests so that her two sons could watch the eggs hatch. She showed it to one of her naturalist friends, who informed us that it was not eggs, but the aptly named bird's nest fungus (*Cyathus striatus* or a related species). Though we were disappointed that the eggs weren't going to hatch, I was glad to find a fungus that could be positively identified.

At least seven different types of umbrella-shaped mushrooms appeared in my garden, but I wasn't able to positively identify any of them. However, my mushroom guide has proven useful on hikes, when I've found hen-of-the-woods, morels, and earth stars, among others.

In my search for descriptions of bugs and their habits, I ran across another treasure in a used bookstore. <u>The Wildlife Gardener</u> by John V. Dennis, in the course of explaining how to attract wildlife to any garden, describes all sorts of creatures, their behavior, and habitats or plants in or on which they might be found. Dennis addresses mammals and insects, reptiles and amphibians, with equal curiosity and reverence for all.

I was transfixed on reading Dennis' account of the hummingbird moth (*Hemaris thysbe*). A member of the sphinx moth tribe, it is so named because its wings beat as quickly as a hummingbird's, and it drinks nectar with its long tongue. I read about it with some wistfulness, thinking how unlikely I was to meet one, and wishing for the umpteenth time that I owned an enormous property encompassing a wide range of habitats, so that I could explore and meet new animals.

Several weeks later, I stood on my new Exposed Bedrock Patio one evening at dusk, smelling the intensified sweetness of the butterfly bushes. I heard a loud buzzing, then a creature the size of a monarch butterfly zipped into view and hovered over one of the buddleia flowers, its wings blurred from beating so fast. I squinted in the dim light and saw black and yellow wings and a pink- and red-striped body. The creature's long tongue unrolled and penetrated one of the flowers. I watched it sup for ten or fifteen minutes until it flitted off into the night.

Was it a dream? A bizarre coincidence? Or had the hummingbird moth been visiting my garden regularly, unnoticed, before I read Dennis' description of it?

I'm puzzled that moths inspire indifference or even repugnance in many people, while butterflies, which overlap moths in look and habit, elicit unanimous wonder and appreciation. Most gardeners' guides either ignore moths or mention only the spectacular handful that includes the luna and sphinx, while butterflies are well-documented; butterfly guidebooks abound for novice and experienced observers, and general garden books often devote sections to attracting butterflies and meeting their needs during every season.

A good beginner's book is The Butterfly Book by Donald and Lillian Stokes and Ernest Williams. It allowed me to identify the eight or ten common species of butterfly that visited my garden during the first few years. Then I started noticing smaller species that may have been moths, and that weren't covered in the book. I also ran across caterpillars I couldn't find in the guide. I haven't yet found a guide to butterflies, moths, and caterpillars that can hold a candle to my mushroom encyclopedia.

In a city garden, flying animals are more likely visitors than creeping or slithering ones. The reptiles were not represented at all in my little plot, and the only mammals I saw that weren't domesticated were squirrels and the occasional rabbit.

The most noticeable—and by far the best-documented—garden animals are the birds. I was able to identify every species that I saw in my garden with help from Stan Tekiela's <u>Birds of Minnesota Field Guide</u>. This small but comprehensive book covers bird species whose migratory range includes Minnesota. It provides color photographs of male and female adults for each species, organized by primary color and cross-referenced. It also maps migration patterns and notes the time of year the birds are likely to be in Minnesota, which helped me spot them and connect them with the local seasonal rhythm.

During the Winter-to-Spring and Fall-to-Winter transitions, bands of migrating juncos visited to scour the patio rocks for ants. In early Spring, a yellow-breasted warbler dallied among the forsythia flowers. In Summer, a downy woodpecker hopped up the white birch trunk and a shy house wren flitted through the ankles of the shrubs. Cardinals lived in my neighborhood year-round, taking long, luxurious baths, but their calls changed with the seasons.

I was pleased whenever I noticed a new animal in the garden. On the wall in my front porch, I tacked up two lists, one of the bird species seen in my garden and one of the butterflies. Beside each species name I wrote the year in which I first saw it. A couple of new species appeared on each list every year. In the first Summer, I listed 10 bird species and 3 butterfly or moth species. By the fourth Summer, those numbers grew to 22 and 10. Someday, when I can identify more of them, I hope to add lists of insects and fungi, those under-appreciated visitors who add so much interest to my garden.

Filling Gaps
(Fourth Winter)

"Normally many different plants live together, filling a variety of niches—some provide shade and shelter, others ground cover; some are permanent residents, others ever-ready to fill spaces that become available; some are active at one season, others at another."

Peter Thompson, <u>The Self-Sustaining Garden</u>

Fill a gallon jar with big rocks and people think it's full, then add gravel, which sifts down between the rocks, and they marvel at your cleverness, then add sand and they shake their heads because it's certainly full now, then add water. My garden was like that, and my friends and neighbors reacted to it just as people do on first seeing the jar trick.

I would praise a new bush or tree I'd just planted, and someone would say, "Another bush? How did you fit it in?" Someone else would ask, "How large does it get?" I learned to expect their disbelief. Like that gallon jar, my garden contained more elements than people considered possible.

A naturalistic style of planting mingles trees, grasses, perennials, annuals, and shrubs in the same planting beds, with a few vines growing among them for good measure. In ecological terms, my garden would be classed as "edge" habitat, a transition zone between wooded and open areas. Edge habitats are often richer in diversity and denser in growth than surrounding areas. They can support some plants from each of the adjacent communities as well as some plants that don't grow in either community.

For instance, where a forest borders a prairie, there will coexist forest trees and prairie grasses, plus a host of shrubs found in neither mid-forest nor mid-prairie. The edge conditions perfectly suit this shrub layer, offering enough shade that the prairie plants form sparser communities among which shrub roots can take hold, but enough sun that the shrubs can thrive.

Not only were my garden's plants layered in space, they were also layered in time. Bulbs and early-blooming perennials (sometimes called ephemerals) bloomed in Spring and died back, and in late Spring, perennials and more bulbs grew up in their places, and later in the Summer, a third group shouldered fresh, sturdy stems up through the dying foliage of their predecessors.

Like Mary Poppins' carpetbag, the garden expanded to hold all the plants I offered it. Certain areas supported so many plants that I couldn't keep track of them, and on peering into their midst, I often met one I'd forgotten about, or another that had self-sowed unexpectedly.

At the end of the third Summer, I tried to count the plants and the different species in my front garden. I'd managed to fit roughly 40 individual trees and shrubs, 200 perennials and vines, and 300 bulbs—in all, about 65 species or varieties—into about 500 square feet of space. And still, enough bare mulch remained to support more plants. Gaps occurred where plants died or grew smaller than expected, in bare circles around the legs of new shrubs, in areas where plants emerged early and then died back, and in areas where plants emerged late.

I planned to fill the gaps. The first step was to re-read my two garden journals.

I'd started a journal the first Summer when I realized I couldn't expect George to listen to every detail of my plans, every scrap of new information about each plant, and a thorough description of every garden feature I coveted. The journal began with a self-conscious note that it wouldn't be that interesting to read, but would be a receptacle for ideas and observations to which I could refer later. Then I listed the plant characteristics I wanted to track annually, effused for two pages about the early bulbs that were coming up, and contradicted myself by scribbling, "I take it back—this is a fascinating book!"

The first volume was full of exclamations, discoveries, and poetic descriptions. Buried among these ravings were the Latin names of the plants I bought and where I planted them. At the end of the Summer, I walked around my garden and listed what was growing in each area, described its seasonal and spatial gaps, and noted ideas for improvement. At the back of the journal, I kept a list of things to do in the garden. By Fall, the list numbered 77 items and the journal was filled.

I was glad I'd recorded the scientific names of plants and saved their tags and my receipts. That helped when I wanted to find more of a particular plant. I was also glad I'd written where things were planted, since the plants didn't die back or emerge at the same time every year, and if I planted when they weren't showing above-ground, it was easy to accidentally dig up a late-rising perennial or damage an early bulb.

However, the more pages I filled, the harder it became to hunt through what I'd written for the name of a plant or a description of what plants grew in a certain area. Before long, I was wishing for better-organized records about where plants had come from, how big they were when first planted, and why they died or were moved.

I started volume two of my garden journal during the first Winter, and this time I tried to organize the information so it would be easier to use. To compare bloom and leaf times from year to year, I made a calendar to annually track bloom, leaf-out, Autumn color change, and berry and seed formation dates. This would help me plan overlaps and combinations. I also made a list of plants I'd tried and especially liked, and wrote why I liked them, hoping it would help me learn to choose plants more wisely.

Before I filled the second book, I had decided that I wanted to make a notebook to serve as a plant reference for my garden. It would include each plant's physical description, photographs or pictures from catalogs, a brief history of my experiences with growing and propagating it, and snippets of information or "lore" that I ran across in my reading (such as origins of common names, medicinal uses, edibility, and preferred plant companions).

This notebook of individual plant information, along with the bloom and leaf calendar and the annual descriptions of each area in my garden, would one day help me to fill gaps with deliberation and artistic finesse. But while I was collecting the data, I chose two easy strategies for quickly covering the ground with plants. These strategies were bulbs and propagation.

Many of my perennials (asters, blackeyed Susans, coreopsis, butterfly weed) were prairie plants that didn't emerge until late Spring or early Summer. Over and among them, I planted chinodoxa and crocus; these bulbs would bloom first, then their brown dying leaves would be eclipsed by the fresh green foliage of the perennials.

Unfortunately, I bought 50 giant crocus on sale instead of choosing the smaller, wilder-looking ones that weren't on sale, so every year when the crocus came up, I wistfully compared their ungainly garish purple funnels to the delicate lavender flowers of my few smaller crocus. Luckily for me, the big crocus are short-lived and a delectable treat for squirrels, so their numbers shrank every year.

My woodland was carpeted with ladyferns (*Athyrium filix-femina*), and they came up after the miniature *Narcissus* finished blooming; I added more mini *Narcissus* among the ferns, and I also added windflowers (*Anemone blanda*) among them for an even earlier season. They're short and cornflower blue, with flat, open faces like daisies, and trios of small triangular scalloped leaves. I wanted them to cover the ground under the jack pine, but a crafty squirrel followed my tracks and dug up a good number of them. It turned out that he had only rearranged them, though, for the next Spring, many of the windflowers came up in my lawn and neighboring lawns. Enough remained in the woodland bed to create a pleasing succession of windflowers to yellow narcissus to ferns.

Bulbs can fill spatial gaps too. Where low masses of sweet woodruff grew along the side path, I planted a dozen bulbs of a late-Spring-blooming species tulip (*Tulipa turkestanica*). This tulip's nearly leafless stems emerge through the sweet woodruff foliage in May. Each stem throws out multiple flowers. The blooms are yellow with white bands down the center of each petal, and the five petals spread out like nearly flat stars. They look more like miniature Asiatic lilies than tulips. By the time the sweet woodruff thrusts up its own tiny white star-flowers in June, the tulip blooms have dried into decorative brown pods on stiff tan stalks.

The other quick method I used for filling gaps was propagating plants that already grew in my garden. The Maple Grove experience helped me come to somewhat shaky terms with my lust for variety, so when I noticed a gap my first thought was no longer, "Which new plant off my list would fill this gap?" but "Which existing plant could be spread into this gap?" Propagated plants had a great chance of thriving; their parents had proven they were adapted to the conditions of the garden.

Propagating was easy with plants that already self-sowed in my garden. I simply dropped their ripe seeds where I wanted them to appear. As for those that spread by forming larger masses of stems, I dug a shovel into the mass and divided them to get extra plants. This worked on suckering shrubs too.

However, some plants—bushes in particular—weren't easy to propagate by division or seeds. In these cases, I felt I could justify buying more. Alas, even when I'd written down the exact name of a plant I'd bought, I wasn't sure to find more of it later. Most local nurseries stock a few classics and the latest hybrids, and earlier years' offerings fall by the wayside.

When I mulched the grassy, south-facing front slope, I planned to plant more 'Texas Scarlet' flowering quinces there. I had bought one the previous year and liked its vicious thorns and gracefully twisted shape. It flowered with bright red blossoms early each Spring. The thorns discouraged cats and dogs from disturbing birds and squirrels that might hide within it.

I found no 'Texas Scarlets' that year, however, nor any other flowering quinces. The nursery that had sold it to me said they received complaints about its hardiness, so they stopped carrying it. Flowering quinces had also disappeared from the catalogs. Though my own bush looked happy and healthy, it didn't occur to me to try propagating other plants from it. Instead, I bought red and gold Japanese barberries and low, spreading evergreens for the slope.

I was reading Christopher Lloyd's The Well-tempered Garden, a section of which described woody propagation techniques and the plants on which Lloyd had tried them. This kind of propagation didn't interest me. Snipping stems in just the right way would lead me from the garden, my playground, back into the world of right and wrong, manuals and procedures, which I'd rather avoid on my days off work.

I half-skimmed the text as Lloyd described a method for snipping foot-long segments of certain plants and pushing them into the ground in Autumn. They'd create roots and leaf out the next Spring. He wrote that plants propagated from cuttings flowered earlier and grew faster than plants started from seed. A shortcut, I thought, and paid closer attention.

He hooked me when he mentioned how well this method worked for butterfly bushes (*Buddleia davidii*). I happened to love my two buddleias and was tempted to buy others, but although (unlike the quince) they were still available at nurseries, the price seemed high and my willingness to pay high prices for plants was fading as my garden filled.

Propagation was sounding more interesting. If I could make more butterfly bushes, I would spread them around lavishly. My garden would become a butterfly paradise. Perhaps I should try Lloyd's method before I dismissed it as too difficult.

I walked outside one frosty December day and took cuttings off the woody branches of my buddleias. The weather was unusual that year, and a warm spell had caused the buddleias, which died off every Fall, to leaf out again prematurely. The frost then stopped the small leaves from growing. Eventually they would dry up and fall, but when I cut them, they were alive and tender.

I followed Lloyd's detailed instructions; he suggested "trimming each, top and bottom, just above and just below a node, to make sticks a foot long, which can be stuck by two-thirds their length into light soil". I shoved my cuttings into the soil near the parent plants.

In March, the snow melted from the Exposed Bedrock Patio, and I went out to see if any bulbs were up yet. It was unusually warm and hit 70 degrees Fahrenheit for a couple of days in a row before returning to the customary 20 degrees. Some of the crocus and species tulips were poking cautious leaf-tips above the mulch. In the rich, fertile soil under the jack pine where I'd stuck half a dozen buddleia cuttings, no trace of them survived, but in the lime sand at the edge of the patio, one of my sticks sported several tufts of fuzzy new leaves. I pulled at it to be sure it was alive, and its roots resisted.

I had made a twig grow! It was even more thrilling than growing plants from seed, mainly because it seemed so improbable. I rejoiced in my new shrub's magical birth, then eagerly clipped some branches off the pagoda dogwood, cut them using Lloyd's method, and pushed them into the sand next to the patio.

Nature Includes Humans

"Ecological thinking aims to use all the resources of science to see how life operates and how we can fit responsibly into its patterns."

Ernest Callenbach, <u>Ecology: A Pocket Guide</u>

There weren't many animals in our neighborhood (well, it was the middle of the city), but I was eager to attract them. I wanted to know them better and liked the idea of living on land that supported wildlife. Though I figured our yard was too small to make a difference in the overall scheme of things—to prevent some bird from becoming extinct, for instance—it still might improve the lives of local animals.

I took pains to attract animals into the garden. For birds, I tried to supply year-round food (berries and insects), cover, water, and grit for digestion. For butterflies, I tried to ensure nectar sources throughout the Summer, water and sand for drinking and bathing, and in late Summer, egg-laying sites with larval food sources. I also tried to minimize elements that might repel animals: the smell and taste of pesticides, noise from lawnmowers, disturbances from weeding and clipping.

Since the surrounding yards were so bare, I made my boundary plantings extra-wide and packed them densely, hoping they might draw shier animals like ground-nesting birds and voles. I let shrubs interlace.

As the boundaries of the front garden grew tall and thick with foliage, human visitors became more hesitant. They stayed on the main walk, wary of shadowy corners. They skittered down the side path, through vines and bushes, and were visibly relieved to reach the open parking area and unplanted beds in the backyard.

One would think a lot of foliage is a bad thing.

Well-meaning neighbors and friends offered advice on how I could wrest the land back from the nonhumans:

"You'll want to trim that forsythia; it's sticking up over the fence."

"Looks like squirrels have been digging in your mulch. Have you tried blood meal?"

"You shouldn't put wood chips near your hostas. You'll get slugs."

Apparently many people don't agree that we've gone overboard in segregating ourselves from other species.

However, at various times during my life, I have felt like I belong in the natural world, one of the plants and animals, not just an alien observer. I wanted to feel that sense of belonging in my garden. Humans and animals can coexist, can't they?

I was puzzling this question while I installed edging bricks to separate the last two pieces of my front lawn from the adjacent planting beds. I meant to edge the front beds when I made them, but it seemed like such a minor detail that I neglected it in order to make more beds and plant more plants. Now, I was hoping to curb the nefarious creeping Charlie that had overtaken the lawn and harbored designs on the beds.

I found the perfect edging bricks at the landscape supply yard where I'd bought my rocks. The cement edgers were colored pale mustard, a hue also present in the limestone that now jutted up from so many parts of my garden that it looked indigenous. They were six inches long with one end slanted and one straight, so they could be fitted end-to-end in a curve or a straight line. Along the length of each brick's underside, a deep vee dissected two lower edges. My theory about this unusual shape was that plants that tried to creep under them would be fooled into pushing their stems up into the vee, where they'd exhaust their energy trying to break through the brick to the surface, never figuring out that they must go back down and then up again to reach it.

The landscape supply yard also sold a long skinny spade just wider than the bricks, with which I dug a ditch around the boundaries between bed and lawn, then spread an inch of sand at the bottom and settled the bricks in the sand, all in an afternoon.

I was surprised that George noticed the edging bricks right away and even more surprised at how much he liked them.

"They make it feel more finished," he said. "Why don't you put them around the front patio too, and the beds in back?"

George only offers suggestions about the garden when he feels strongly about something. I value his ideas, which are usually elegant in a way that mine are not, maybe because I cater to the tastes of birds and butterflies rather than people. I've even grown fond of the garish purple-leaf sand cherries he picked out; they offer an interesting change from green-leaved shrubs, their graceful vase shapes require minimal pruning, their shell-pink flowers stand out against their deep rosy-purple foliage, and they're hardy to zone 3.

George enjoys animal watching and loved our garden's abundant foliage, so I was kind of disappointed when he said he wanted all the areas to have edges. Must a garden show overt signs of human intention to be attractive to people?

Until then, I hadn't thought much about whether other people would like my garden. I figured animal lovers would recognize its value, and those who focused on floral displays would find it dull and overgrown. Now I wondered if there was a way to make a garden that felt wild enough to me and the animals, but also appealed to (or at least didn't repulse) other people.

It could be an interesting challenge, to make my garden comfortable enough for human visitors without rescinding my invitation to animals. If I could do it, it might demonstrate how people could live closer to wildlife without giving up a beautiful garden.

If George's tastes were typical, then a distinct edge around the wild areas would help. And Michael the landscape consultant had mentioned balancing the foliage with open areas. What else might make people feel safe and relaxed in a wilder garden?

I recalled hiking along a state forest path that suddenly emerged into a streamside clearing and spotting a welcome bench on which to rest and watch the water. I remembered dozing in a bed of long grass on a hill covered with daisies. Reading a book on a large flat rock in the middle of a river. Savoring a campfire-roasted hot dog with my back against a tall evergreen, seated on a soft mat of pine needles.

Maybe seating was the missing element.

My garden issued no invitations to sit and enjoy it, unless I counted the rotting benches that matched the picnic table we'd used for firewood several years back. Perhaps Cassandra Danz was right in saying: "Every garden room should have a place to sit. Without a place to sit, it's not a room, it's a vestibule." Perhaps this also explained why I didn't spend much time relaxing in my garden.

I paged through catalogs, looking at pictures of benches and chairs. The pieces were expensive, and given my garden's small size, furniture wouldn't fit into every one of its rooms. And though I would like to have seating in the wilder areas of the garden so people would spend more time there, chairs and benches would take away much of the wildness.

Maybe I could use raised, flat surfaces that would cost less and look more natural. Instead of a bench in the Woodland Clearing, I imagined three log slices of different heights grouped together—tall for a seat, medium for a table, and low for a footstool. Other ideas included a fallen log, a stump covered with moss, a wide wall, a flat rock, a low tree branch, a swing, or a hammock.

I pondered some more. Seating might relax my human visitors, but how would I entice them into sitting? I needed obvious, sturdy paths to guide visitors to each seat. Once there, I hoped they'd be comfortable enough to linger and notice the scent of leaves and flowers, the sounds of rustling and chirping, the texture of nearby surfaces. Maybe they'd discover (or rediscover) how relaxing, entertaining, and sensually pleasing nature could be. Maybe they'd be inspired to welcome more plants and animals to their own land.

I worry about wildlife, about fragmented and disappearing habitats, about extinction of species, about decreased biodiversity and increased urbanization and deforestation and what they mean for the future climate and stability of the earth. But I also worry about people.

My mom, who grew up on a family farm, told me that she used to lie in the corrugates—the ditches between planted rows in a field—and stare up at the waving wheat. She still uses this memory to relax herself in times of stress. What becomes of children who have no such memories of pleasurably losing themselves among plants and animals, of not being human but transcending humanness and just being?

Rustic camping, family farming, stargazing—these experiences are becoming rarer. How many people have waded alone into a remote lake under a full moon? How many have met a wolf on an isolated ski trail? How many can regularly see the night sky? How many have sensed the largeness, the awesomeness, of nature and sought refuge there from their own smallness and isolation? How many have linked nature with God, appreciation with prayer?

I've watched the transformation of fields, woods, and wetlands to housing and shopping developments with a growing sense of unease and helplessness. When I read books like <u>Noah's Garden</u> by Sara Stein and <u>Second Nature</u> by Michael Pollan and <u>Why We Garden</u> by Jim Nollman, I feel hopeful that gardens can replace some of what we've lost to development—not just habitat for animals and plants, but also people's daily experience of nature. Persuading people to see their gardens in this role could change a significant fraction of the American landscape.

Cynics may wonder if it's possible to change the landscape of an entire country by changing people's ideas about gardening. It's been done. Landscape architect Ian McHarg describes how a new way of thinking about landscapes transformed the British countryside in the eighteenth century: "Starting with a denuded landscape, a backward agriculture, and a medieval pattern of attenuated land holdings, this landscape tradition rehabilitated the entire countryside, making that fair image persisting today. It is a testimony to the prescience of William Kent, Lancelot 'Capability' Brown, Humphry Repton, and their followers that... they used native plant materials to create communities which so well reflected natural processes that their creations endured and are self-perpetuating."

We in the United States are a long way from living in a self-perpetuating landscape. We drape our outdoor environments in lawn; it's not only our choice for play areas, but our default for areas where we don't have another plan. We maintain our lawns by mowing, fertilizing, and killing off encroaching plants (weeds) and animals (pests). Without our continued intervention, these lawns would cease to exist.

A growing number of people have a different vision of an ideal landscape, one that includes more plant and animal species and assigns humans a less controlling role with respect to other species. In <u>Planting</u>

<u>Noah's Garden</u>, Sara Stein explores how suburban gardeners could change the character of the American landscape. This sequel to <u>Noah's Garden</u> offers plans for transforming a modest suburban lot so it will support more wildlife and provide more emotional and sensory fulfillment to its owners. In <u>The Wildlife Gardener</u>, John V. Dennis gives persuasive evidence that suburban gardens, properly planted and managed, can actually support more wildlife than some wild areas.

Governments, corporations, schools, and golf courses are exploring the benefits (aesthetic, environmental, and financial) of landscaping with native plants, restoring natural communities, and preserving existing natural areas. Scientific research has begun to corroborate that time spent among plants and animals offers psychological benefits to people, including increased calm, reduced violence, and refreshed ability to concentrate.

My garden showed me how daily experience of the natural world sustains my mental, emotional, physical, and spiritual health. I suspected it might urge other people toward the same realization.

To that end, I began introducing visitors to individual plants and animals. I offered bits of my garden for them to taste or touch. I handed them leaves of chocolate mint to chew. I broke open the papery seedpods from the love-in-a-puff vines (*Cardiospermum halicacabum*) and showed off the heart-shaped marks on the seeds that give the plant its common name. I encouraged visitors to taste leaves of lavender, garden sage, sweet woodruff, anise hyssop (*Agastache foeniculum*), oregano, and thyme, to stroke the silky rose petals, to crouch and inhale the sweet fragrance of the violets, to watch the evening sun glowing through the milky blooms of the musk mallow. I served tea made from garden plants as we watched the charades of insects, squirrels, and birds. I shared my lists of animal visitors with neighbors and friends. I offered plants to other gardeners and encouragement and ideas (when they asked) for their own wild landscapes.

We gain so much by accommodating nature: entertainment, connection, awe, joy, humor, perspective, peace. It is a small step, making connections between the people I know and the plants and animals I harbor, but doing it relieves some of my frustration. Though nature is disappearing from the larger landscape, it (humans included) is invited to live in my small patch of paradise.

Paradise Emerges
(Fourth Summer)

"Americans are gradually becoming more conscious of the need for enclosure, a concept prevalent in other, often older cultures, who for centuries have lived in close proximity to each other."

Julie Messervy, <u>The Inward Garden</u>

As the fourth Summer approached, my enthusiasm for gardening waned. The plants were growing slower than I'd hoped. Our small hedges created a psychological boundary for adults but were ignored by dogs and children, who barreled through the bushes in pursuit of balls, squirrels, and each other.

We decided to move things along by building the wooden fence we'd discussed during our first few months in the house. It would instantly increase our privacy while we waited for the plants to mature, and it would be a more solid barrier than even full-grown shrubs could provide.

Aesthetics also figured in the decision. A fence would create a crisp frame to balance my exuberant plantings, an effect whose success was foreshadowed by the brick edging. Its untreated cedar would age to a gray that complemented the plant colors and matched the existing trellis, and it would block out views of cars, other houses, and pedestrians, providing a restful background against which to contemplate the garden.

The need for enclosure is not universally understood. Carol Williams writes: "I grew up in England, where garden walls are considered only polite, and live now in an American community where they are illegal. I could laugh at this paradox if I did not also feel it in myself."

I think part of the general antipathy toward enclosure has to do with the view. People often want to see as far as possible—is it to feel safer from predators, I wonder, or to feel connected to their surroundings, or to maximize sunlight, or something else altogether? Even if the view isn't a landscape, but a streetscape of houses and cars and pedestrians (or the interior of the neighbor's house), many prefer it to an enclosed space.

A friend told me about a man she knew who lived alone in a house next door to an elderly woman. The woman scolded him several times for walking through his dining room in his underwear. Her kitchen windows afforded a clear view of his dining room, and his indecent displays bothered her. The man didn't enjoy her watching him either, so he built a deck outside his dining room, and on the far side of the deck, he built a high wooden wall. The woman complained bitterly that his wall blocked her view.

My neighbor also preferred a view to privacy, as I'd learned by her strong reaction to my initial pergola plan, which would have blocked the view between her kitchen and our dining room. I would guess that most of our neighbors shared her preference, though they were unfailingly polite when our fence came up in conversation.

The fence was an even more radical departure for our neighborhood than the front Woody Border had been. Every other front yard within several blocks was entirely visible from the street. The handful of other front fences were either expedient chain link installed to contain the resident dog or elegant wrought iron to emphasize the house.

If I'd been a gardener when we were house-shopping, I wouldn't have chosen that particular house or the role of fence pioneer. I might have passed over that neighborhood to find one in which large, private gardens were the norm. Instead, I was stuck wondering if and how I should try to justify our new private landscape to residents who'd probably chosen the neighborhood (decades ago) for its open front yard scheme.

I didn't expect to persuade people to my point of view, though it would have been a welcome relief if someone had confessed to also valuing nature and outdoor privacy. I just thought explaining myself would more likely mend our relations with neighbors than would sitting quietly behind my new fence. However, I must admit that I did a lot of the latter, and did it blissfully.

The fence renewed my enthusiasm for the garden. It was such a relief to spend time outdoors unobserved. That Summer, I lounged for hours in my paradise-in-progress, thinking and writing.

My desire to experience the garden had outstripped my drive to build more of it. Instead of hauling, pounding, and digging during my spare time, I sat and watched the birds and insects, examined the individual plants and the various views.

My urgent lists of things to do metamorphosed into paragraphs that explored several ways of filling a gap, or the different places to which I might move an unhappy plant. The paragraphs were tentative; sentences started with "maybe" and ended in question marks. I felt less pressure to decide among the alternatives and was inclined to gather them and mull them over until I found the energy to act.

Sporadically, I worked on the back yard skeleton. I edged the parking area with old railroad ties whose sere, solid bulk fit with the large shrubs and broad sweeps of plants that would fill the adjacent planting beds. Taking George's advice, I edged these beds with the same bricks I'd used in front. I extended the side path into the backyard, branching it around the old vegetable bed to meet the parking area on one side and the future back patio on the other.

I planned to spread lime gravel over the future patio, parking area, and new path, then add stepping stones and paving as budget and energy allowed. My energetic grandma came to visit again just after the gravel was delivered—six cubic yards of it—and she wouldn't be satisfied until she and I had spread the whole pile. This took us several days, since we had to rest between bouts of shovel and barrow work. It was harder than pulling off dandelion heads.

Lime gravel is sharp-edged, and rainfall will gradually compact it into a cement-like shell if it's kept clear of seedlings. To keep perennial weeds from coming up through it, I laid down plastic tarps before spreading the gravel. I didn't want to use plastic, but my other choices were applying weed-killer or renting a compacting roller. Plastic seemed cheapest and quickest and promised the least work.

After a week or so, the gravel settled. It no longer shifted underfoot or sent up dust, and it gave the backyard an arid look foreign to this lush region. But it matched the limestone rocks and didn't look unnatural.

I hoped that it would prove to be a marriage of the practical and the aesthetic, and that it would make a solid enough surface for the parking area that we wouldn't need to use cement or asphalt.

George ventured into the yard more often that Summer, and we ate dinners seated in our lawn chairs on the patio-to-be. Evening hours were prime hunting time for mosquitoes, which have been dubbed the state bird of Minnesota because they are so numerous and vicious. Wasps also pestered us, swarming around our food and drinks.

To address these problems, I started to wrestle with plans for a summerhouse, to be located in the area I had labeled the Haven. A roofed shelter with screened walls would be expensive and take a while to build by myself, but I came up with several interesting modular designs. Maybe I could enlist some friends to help build it, friends who hadn't helped us move the front patio rocks. Had any of our friends not heard that story yet?

George put an end to this agony of planning when he went shopping one morning and returned with a screen tent, big enough to stand up inside, small enough that one person could set it up alone. This option hadn't occurred to me.

We set up the screen tent in the spot that I'd slated for the summerhouse, and we didn't take it down all Summer, except to replace it with the deluxe model, which allowed us to have outdoor dinners with a couple of friends, or to sit out a rainstorm together, just the two of us, huddled in the protected center.

In the meantime, I tinkered with the plantings around our new Exposed Bedrock Patio. To make the enormous rock slabs blend into the landscape and appear older, I planted mother-of-thyme (*Thymus serpyllum*) and wooly thyme (*T. pseudolanuginosis*) in the sandy pockets between them. Nature contributed scattered violets and two creeping plants that eked out their lives in the sidewalk cracks. One was two to three inches high and dense with round dark green leaves. In Fall, it turned a deep maroon that matched the Fall color of the nearby rhododendron. The other plant was flat and sent out well-spaced branches that formed a rough grid pattern. Each branch carried small leaves of fresh green, and in Summer, tiny white star-shaped flowers. Both creepers were welcome to as much of the new patio as they could usurp.

On the slightly raised banks around the patio, I planted thirty creeping phlox (*P. subulata*) in various colors interspersed with more creeping thyme. I envisioned this informal edging of creepers as a gradual transition between the patio and planting beds, though I hoped the creepers would also serve the practical purpose of edging—keeping the wood chips from washing onto the rocks with every hard rainfall.

I ordered the creeping phlox from a wholesale nursery that sold in quantity to individuals as well as businesses. The minimum order was ten plants. The price, something like a quarter apiece for two-inch pots, catapulted creeping phlox to the top of my list of desirable groundcovers. I saved the time and energy of growing groundcovers from seed, and I paid less than a third of what I might have through a retail catalog and probably a tenth of what a garden center would have charged for the plants.

I also bought two Siberian cypresses (*Microbiota decussata*) for the front patio area. Dark green feathery leaves drooped from their main stems, which curved back on themselves in a low, flat circle. These evergreens were ultra-hardy, to Zone 2, and would grow slowly into four-foot-diameter thickets only a foot high. They were the first plants I had to wear gloves to handle.

I selected them at the nursery, hoisted them onto one of the little green wagons, and after they'd been purchased, lifted them into the trunk of my car. As I drove home, I looked down at my bare arms and saw a bright red rash where my skin had brushed against the cypress leaves. I'd read about this happening with certain plants. At home, I pulled on a sweatshirt and gloves and planted the cypresses, averting my face from their waving leaves and hoping that this wasn't some poison ivy-like allergy that would spread across my body.

The rash vanished by the next day. The cypresses made up for that passing discomfort by turning wine-purple in the Autumn, which was coincidentally the same color as the nearby rhododendron and the unidentified groundcover. By another happy coincidence, I could meditate on this scene from my front porch, and I spent the chill days of Autumn and Winter thus, until it was buried under the undiscriminating snow.

How a Gardener Grows

"Those who do not know are apt to think that hardy flower gardening of the best kind is easy. It is not easy at all. It has taken me half a lifetime merely to find out what is best worth doing, and a good slice out of another half to puzzle out the ways of doing it."

Gertrude Jekyl, from a 1911 article entitled "Colour Scheme in the Flower Garden", quoted in <u>Virago Book of Women Gardeners</u>

Every year I refined my garden at a smaller level of detail. The work wasn't likely to stop during my lifetime, but the type of work was changing. I wasn't planting as much, or hauling rocks or laying gravel.

I was weeding a lot. And still filling gaps. When I thought an area was full, another possibility would occur to me, or one of the resident plants would sicken, die, or outgrow its space and need to be replaced.

I started to wonder, would this be my future role? When I finished laying out the garden and planting it, would I simply maintain it for years, weeding and filling gaps, caring for plants and arranging them in compatible groups? Had I dug and coddled and sweated and memorized, all to become a servant of my own garden?

The red tulips bloomed and answered my questions.

I didn't choose the red tulips. They were a free gift for buying so many bulbs at a nursery. I planted them on the front slope because I thought dog-walkers might enjoy a bright clump of bloom so close to the sidewalk after viewing countless foundation plantings across bare lawns.

When the red tulips bloomed, they set off the dark purple leaves and pink flowers of the sand cherry behind them. A splash of yellow from the spiraeas below highlighted their redness. I hadn't planned the effect, hadn't given any thought to matching the tulips with their surroundings, since they would only bloom for a couple of weeks in Spring and would likely die out after a few years.

I kept walking out to the sidewalk to stare at them.

I hadn't understood why garden authors rave about plant combinations. I hadn't foreseen the singing in the blood, the mixture of pride and awe that comes from hosting a stunning combination. I felt mild delight when my rhododendron and cypress and unidentified groundcover all turned the same shade of purple, but this new combination was a blend of complementary and contrasting colors, flowers, and foliage. It was art.

I remembered reading that red tulips set off the first red shoots of peonies and finish blooming before the peony foliage obscures them. Though I'd given away more than half of them, a patch of double pink peonies still dominated one area of the garden. I planted red tulips among them one Autumn.

When Spring came, the peony shoots grew and leafed out so quickly they threatened to engulf the emerging tulips. I wondered if, in another part of the country, tulips bloom earlier in relation to peonies. Or if my mulch slowed the tulips' growth. Maybe a different variety of red tulip was required.

The next Spring, the combination worked just as expected: the peony leaves stayed low until the tulips had bloomed, then grew up to hide the fading tulip leaves. Did the tulips take a year to adjust their schedule, or would their timing vary enough to produce the sought-after effect only sporadically? I couldn't know until I saw more Springs arrive in the garden.

Joe Eck writes in <u>Elements of Garden Design</u>: "Plants make their most forceful contribution to a garden not through their flowers, or even through their foliage, but through their shapes." His discussion of shapes gave me the idea to plant veronicas in front of a dwarf spruce; this pairing became one of my favorite garden scenes. The veronicas' fuzzy purple tapers mimicked the dense shape of the evergreen, making both more noticeable. I added a further echo with low spikes of lavenders.

Another of my favorite combinations involved a mass of lady's mantle (*Alchemilla mollis* 'Thriller') under the river birch, threaded through with yellow perennial foxgloves (*Digitalis lutea*). The effect was a study in contrasts. The narrow leaves of the *Digitalis* were shiny and smooth, while the ruffled, round *Alchemilla* leaves were dull and fuzzy. Their flowers contrasted too; long stalks of pale yellow bells rose up through clouds of tiny lime green blooms. The birch bark, pink tinted and somewhat ragged with dark brown markings, introduced a contrasting texture and color, but the yellow flowers of the two perennials subtly tied the scene together.

Other art experiments were less successful. I'd studied my Mellow Yellow® spiraea almost daily since planting it. I knew its color during different times of the day—the soft glow of morning and evening brought out the lime-green highlights I liked, while the harsher midday sun erased most of the green, so it glowed gold. I knew its habit, a tidy three-foot mound of fine leaves. So when I planted two more Mellow Yellows® under the nearby white birch, I could picture the effect in my mind. But afternoon shade dulled the new bushes' foliage, leaving a mere hint of lime. The fewer, longer branches that they sent out to catch more light spoiled their attractive roundness. I didn't know this shrub as well as I'd thought.

I didn't know much, really, despite four years of obsessed gardening, and my list of things to learn kept getting longer. I wanted to know what conditions make each plant healthy, and what other factors influence its growth, and how plants affect each other's vigor and appearance.

Books contain a lot of information, but they couldn't give detailed instructions for my specific plants and places. My several-year calendar of bloom and leaf was one baby step toward gathering this knowledge. I was also learning as I moved each plant around, trying to give it the right conditions and observing whether it was smothering another plant, or being smothered, or growing in a compatible way.

My garden, in fact, seemed to be a limitless source of information. It spoke in the voices of individual plants—their behavior and health, their sudden appearances and disappearances—and of animals who visited, moved in, or vanished, voting with their feet. These voices told me about the soil, the climate, wind and shade patterns, air and noise pollution levels. I replied through a series of actions—planting, weeding, watering, amending soil, snipping branches and spent flowers. To each of my actions the garden responded by broadcasting more information, to which I replied with more actions, and so forth in a continuing exchange.

If I could learn to notice and interpret those signals from the garden, to pay attention to the subtle signs of health and disease, of rightness and wrongness, then I could gauge the effects of my own actions (and inaction). The garden itself could teach me how to garden.

My bit of land had been growing things since the world began. Each plant knew more about its needs, and about its relationships with other plants and animals, than I did. Microbes in the soil, insects, grubs, and other creatures that I never notice played a role I couldn't grasp. Maybe after years of research and observation, I'd have a more complete understanding of what was happening and how to influence it. But my knowledge was still so rudimentary that I was lucky to deliver plants to places in which they could survive for a season.

I started my garden as the omnipotent landowner, focused on my powers and on all the things I could control. As I worked with my land and got to know it better, though, I came to appreciate its uniquenesses and history and inhabitants. Somehow my role shifted when I realized I didn't know enough to shoulder the responsibility of controlling everything that happened in my garden.

The more I learned about how Nature works, the more cautious I became about controlling too rigidly the mix of plants and animals, for fear of upsetting some delicate balance. Those weeds could be the larval food of a bug I admired, or they could be repelling a pest that would otherwise devour one of my favorite plants. The aphids could provide food for the baby birds whose parents I was trying to entice to nest nearby. Pruning up a tree's branches would let in light and heat and let moisture escape, changing the microclimate under the tree, and that might be better or worse for the plants and animals who lived under the tree, but I'd be wise to figure out which before I pruned. And so on, ad infinitum; relationships I didn't even suspect formed and supported the garden inhabitants I enjoyed. The more I read and observed, the more I saw how everything is connected.

The red tulips reminded me that I, too, am connected. Their unexpected beauty cut through me, past my personality and my humanity, deep to the core of me that knows and celebrates the oneness of all life. I began to believe that my participation in the garden, my appreciation for it, are part of its spirit.

Even an ecological gardener is a designer. Turning my urban lawn into a comparatively self-sufficient, wildlife-friendly landscape isn't just a matter of assembling a bunch of raw materials and handing them over to Nature. It's more about using what Nature teaches, what the garden itself teaches, to make informed design choices.

I hope to make enough good choices that my garden will be healthy, will host a diverse array of animals and plants, and will offer humans comfort *and* red tulip moments.

Front Garden

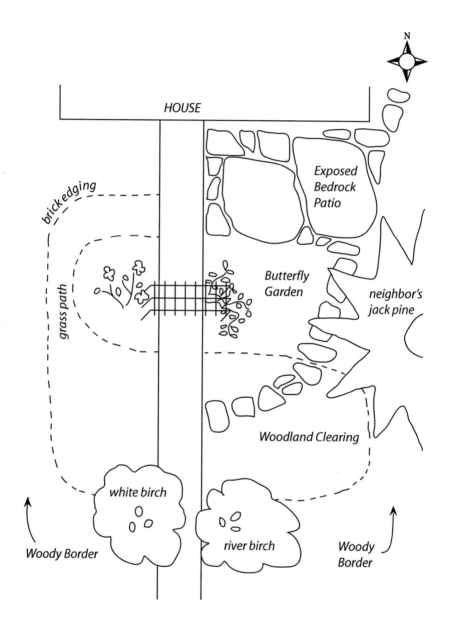

N

HOUSE

brick edging

Exposed
Bedrock
Patio

grass path

Butterfly
Garden

neighbor's
jack pine

Woodland Clearing

white birch

river birch

Woody Border

Woody
Border

Side Garden

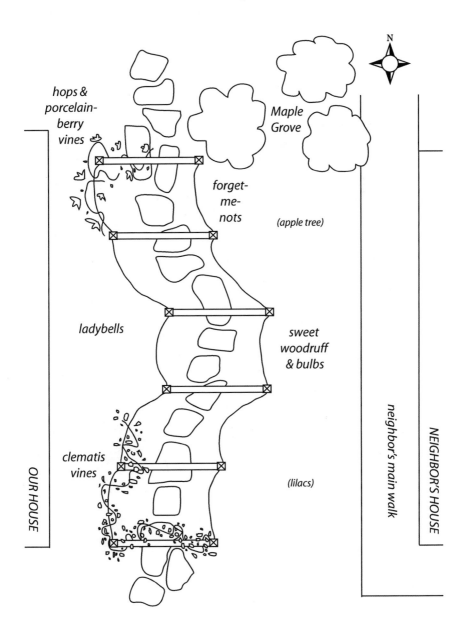

hops &
porcelain-
berry
vines

Maple
Grove

forget-
me-
nots

(apple tree)

ladybells

sweet
woodruff
& bulbs

clematis
vines

(lilacs)

N

neighbor's main walk

NEIGHBOR'S HOUSE

OUR HOUSE

Back Garden

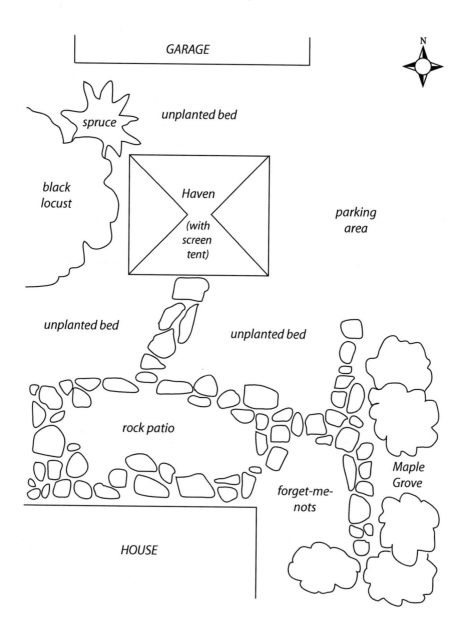

GARAGE

N

spruce

unplanted bed

black
locust

Haven

(with
screen
tent)

parking
area

unplanted bed

unplanted bed

rock patio

Maple
Grove

forget-me-
nots

HOUSE

Sources

Barton, Barbara J. (editor). <u>Taylor's Guide to Specialty Nurseries</u> (Houghton Mifflin, 1993). ISBN: 0395608368
- Now out-of-print, and some of the information is out-of-date. Lists contact information for specialized mail-order nurseries and describes their offerings.

Brookes, John. <u>The Book of Garden Design</u> (MacMillan, 1991). ISBN: 0025166956
- Well-known landscape designer Brookes advocates deciding beforehand what "look" you are aiming for, then building the garden to achieve it. His step-by-step advice at a textbook level of detail guides you through the process of designing a garden. Color photos showcase different styles and components. Diagrams help you choose or develop a design.

Browning, Dominique. <u>Paths of Desire: The Passions of a Suburban Gardener</u> (Scribner, 2004). ISBN: 0743246659
- Browning's original narrative offers a peek into a charming and circuitous mind. Peopled with Helpful Men, the True Love, the Boys, and other characters, the loosely chronological text describes living in the suburbs as a single parent with a demanding job and a dying romance. Portrays the relationship that she developed with her somewhat dilapidated garden over a couple of decades and the comfort she drew from it during times of personal turmoil.

Callenbach, Ernest. <u>Ecology: A Pocket Guide</u> (University of California Press: Pocket edition, 1998). ISBN: 0520214633
- Callenbach's dictionary of ecological concepts covers fire, growth, sulfur, niche, predation, and more. Manages to convey the depth of an ecological perspective with writing clear enough to be easily understood by non-scientists.

Chotzinoff, Robin. <u>People With Dirty Hands: The Passion for Gardening</u> (Wiley, 1996). ISBN: 0156005158

- Series of unrelated stories featuring oddball gardeners and their outrageous adventures. Includes a chapter on where they find all those ladybugs that they sell in the garden catalogs, and another on rose lovers who steal cuttings from old homes and cemeteries. Chotzinoff writes, "...given the choice, I prefer to write about gardeners. They are much more interesting than real people."

Colborn, Nigel. <u>Shortcuts to Great Gardens</u> (Little, Brown, 1993). ISBN: 0316150525

- Colborn packs this volume with practical steps that will give your garden some of that quality of maturity without the wait. Follow the advice in this book to create a garden that exudes permanence and that will continue to improve in beauty and grandeur.

Crowe, Sylvia. Quoted in <u>Virago Book of Women Gardeners</u> (listed under **Kellaway, Deborah**).

Danz, Cassandra. <u>Mrs. Greenthumbs Plows Ahead: Five Steps to the Drop-Dead Gorgeous Garden of Your Dreams</u> (Crown, 1998). ISBN: 0609802658

- For timid gardeners who worry about how to do it right, Danz delivers motivation to go out and get your hands dirty. She plunges into her garden with verve and vigor, tackling challenges as she goes, and when one technique doesn't work, she laughs and tries something else. In this, her second gardening book, Danz describes visits with famous gardeners and tours of well-known gardens, along with plenty of her own stories about projects in her garden. Very witty, fun to read, peppered with handy one-page project guides like "How to Make a Rusticated Arbor".

Dennis, John V. <u>The Wildlife Gardener</u> (Knopf, 1985). ISBN: 0394535820

- Describes some general requirements for wildlife—water, shelter, nesting sites, food—and how to design them into the home landscape. Discusses the habitat preferences of various animal species from opossums to earthworms. Includes seasonally specific plant recommendations.

Eck, Joe. <u>Elements of Garden Design</u> (Henry Holt, 1996). ISBN: 0805037195

- Eck's indispensable primer presents the key concepts of garden design. His concise, flowing prose clearly expresses ideas that are complex enough to interest gardeners at any level of expertise.

Farrand, John. <u>Insects and Spiders: National Audubon Society Pocket Guide</u> (Knopf, 1988). ISBN: 0394757920

- Devotes a brief page to each of the most common insects and spiders in North America, with brief physical description, color photo, and discussion of eating, mating, and reproductive habits.

Fish, Margery. <u>We Made a Garden</u> (Random House: Modern Library Gardening Series, 2002). ISBN: 0375759476

- The title is at once ironic and triumphant, as Fish and her husband clashed on many issues during their years of sharing a garden. The book is written after his death, and she pays ample tribute to his foresight and logic even as she gleefully pursues many of the ideas he squelched.

Frey, Susan and **Barbara Ellis**. <u>Outdoor Living Spaces: How to Create a Landscape You Can Use and Enjoy</u> (Rodale Press, 1992). ISBN: 0875961320

- Frey and Ellis examine a dozen real-life garden designs for different situations and discuss practical and imaginative aspects of the design process. Their gentle, encouraging pointers will guide you to create a garden you will use and enjoy.

Harrison, George H. <u>The Backyard Bird Watcher: The Classic Guide to Enjoying Wild Birds Outside Your Back Door</u> (Simon & Schuster: Fireside edition, 1988). ISBN: 0671663747

- A second-generation birder and wildlife journalist, Harrison's enthusiasm drives this illustrated (B&W) manual for increasing your garden's bird habitat. The book covers bird observation and photography; profiles a variety of bird habitat gardens; and shows how to make bird feeders, houses, water features, and other keys to a good bird habitat. It's not just about attracting birds, but also about the many ways we can enjoy them.

Henderson, Carrol L. <u>Landscaping for Wildlife</u> (Minnesota State Document Center: Spiral edition, 1987). ISBN: 9999529941

- This book-length publication of the Minnesota Department of Natural Resources presents a detailed discussion of many components of a wildlife-friendly landscape and how to implement them in yards, farms, and large wooded acreages. It provides tables of cultivation requirements for trees, shrubs, and perennials native to the Upper Midwestern U.S., and also rates the plants for their value to wildlife and suggests appropriate uses in the landscape.

Heriteau, Jacqueline. <u>Glorious Gardens : Designing, Creating, Nurturing</u> (Stewart, Tabori, & Chang, 1996). ISBN: 1556704852

- Heriteau delivers on her promise of a book that is "filled with breathtaking garden portraits, whose primary purpose is to release your own creativity." Basic, beautiful introduction to many garden types and topics including kitchen gardens, natural gardens, water gardens, and more. As she discusses each idea or issue, she highlights specific plants and describes what each adds to a design. Many color photos illustrate her points.

Hightshoe, Gary. <u>Native Trees and Shrubs of Eastern North America : A Planting Design Manual for Environmental Designers</u> (Wiley, 1987). ISBN: 0471288799

- In this stellar reference, Hightshoe devotes a two-page spread to each plant, including detailed overview and close-up drawings, a map of the plant's geographic range by county, and a host of useful growth and preference information. Describes form, branching, foliage, flower, and fruit. Gives specifics on preferred habitat such as soil type, moisture, temperature, and associated species. Gauges each plant's tolerance for urban conditions and susceptibility to insects, diseases, and wind. It's a pricey but delectable treat for shrub-lovers, especially those with enough space to try more than a handful of species. Essential for landscape designers who wish to use native woody plants.

Hobhouse, Penelope. <u>Garden Style</u> (Willow Creek Press: Reprint edition, 1997). ISBN: 1572230878

- Discusses the variety of styles a garden can assume, sticking to general principles of form rather than specific materials. Instructive text is balanced by many color photos showing outstanding design features of British and American gardens. Contains many mini-portraits of famous and less widely known gardens of all sizes and styles.

Jekyl, Gertrude. Quoted in <u>Virago Book of Women Gardeners</u> (listed under **Kellaway, Deborah**).

Kellaway, Deborah (editor). <u>Virago Book of Women Gardeners</u> (Virago Press, 2001). ISBN: 1860491537
- Pithy and poetic quotations from leading female gardeners and garden writers over the last two centuries, many excerpted from works that are out-of-print.

Kingsbury, Noel. <u>The New Perennial Garden</u> (Henry Holt, 1996). ISBN: 0805046739
- Kingsbury explores the style of gardening that mingles perennials in a bed, paying attention to their growth habits and matching them accordingly. Includes many specific examples of effective combinations.

Lloyd, Christopher. <u>The Well-tempered Garden</u> (The Lyons Press, 1997). ISBN: 155821593X
- This gruff, opinionated, and informative book is a several-hundred-page stream of advice on which plants to use, for what purpose, and how to maintain and harvest them. Lloyd covers hundreds of specific varieties of perennials, annuals, trees, shrubs, herbs, and vegetables. The book includes detailed suggestions for propagating different kinds of plants.

McHarg, Ian L. and **Frederick R. Steiner** (editors). <u>To Heal the Earth: Selected Writings of Ian L. McHarg</u> (Island Press, 1998). ISBN: 155963573-8
- This scholarly yet readable volume presents a collection of essays by architect and community planner Ian McHarg, with introductions and explanatory notes that place each work within the larger context of the movement toward ecologically sound land use and development. Describes the planning and implementation for many of McHarg's specific projects.

Messervy, Julie Moir. <u>The Inward Garden: Creating a Place of Beauty and Meaning</u> (Little, Brown, 1995). ISBN: 0316567922
- Messervy describes several systems for analyzing a gardener's style, landscape archetypes such as caves and promontories, and landscaping techniques that influence the feel of a place, all with the larger purpose of prompting readers to discover the "big idea" they are trying to

express in their gardens. The inward garden is the reader's imagined garden, and Messervy offers guidance in both conceiving and building it.

Moyle, John and **Evelyn Moyle**. <u>Northland Wild Flowers: A Guide for the Minnesota Region</u> (University of Minnesota Press, 1977). ISBN: 0816613559

- The Moyles' book has long been the standard field reference for woodland, wetland, and prairie wildflowers in the Upper Midwest of the United States. Supplies color photographs and brief descriptions of hundreds of native northern flowering herbaceous plants as well as widespread or naturalized exotics.

Nollman, Jim. <u>Why We Garden: Cultivating a Sense of Place</u> (Henry Holt: Owl Book edition, 1996). ISBN: 080504561-9

- Nollman uses anecdotes and short, almanac-style sections to describe his large country garden. Between these sections, he uses a series of metaphorical gardens to discuss social responsibility, spirituality, and politics. Nollman relates to his garden viscerally as well as intellectually, and he shares ideas about how gardeners can improve their sensory and intuitive communication with Nature.

Osler, Mirabel. <u>A Gentle Plea for Chaos</u> (Arcade, 1998). ISBN: 155970439X

- Osler mingles adult wonder and childlike joy as she describes what happens in her English garden and how she consequently feels and acts. Rather than tying gardening to esoteric matters such as world politics or spirituality, Osler advocates garden practices that will spread her own concrete values: more beauty and more pleasure taken in gardening.

Osler, Mirabel. <u>In the Eye of the Garden</u> (Macmillan: Reprint edition, 1994). ISBN: 0025940651

- More of Osler's rambling garden commentary, loosely arranged into chapters (such as "The Persuasive Oleander") that cannot restrain her nimble and curious mind. Set mainly in the town garden she moved to after her husband died, her stories of present gardening joys and chores are mixed with fond memories.

Pleasant, Barbara. Garden Stone: Creative Landscaping with Plants and Stone (Storey, 2004). ISBN: 1580175449
  • This delightfully well-written, award-winning book covers the aesthetic and practical contributions of stone to a garden, with instructions and advice for designing and building stone walks, steps, and terraces.

Polese, Jean-Mari and **Jean-Louis Lamaison.** The Great Encyclopedia of Mushrooms (Konemann: English edition, 1999). ISBN: 3829017286
  • This useful and thorough reference separates mushrooms into nine groups that share key characteristics. Full color photo of each species is accompanied by its Latin name, edibility, average size, similar species, where it is commonly found, and a detailed physical description including age- and area-related variations.

Pollan, Michael. Second Nature: A Gardener's Education (Atlantic Monthly Press, 1991). ISBN: 0802140114
  • Intellectual in tone, this oft-quoted classic discusses contemporary American gardening in the context of humankind's separation from nature. Pollan proposes that the garden can be a middle ground between the wilderness without people that we idealize and the metropolis without nature that we create.

Stein, Sara. Noah's Garden: Restoring the Ecology of Our Own Back Yards (Houghton Mifflin, 1995). ISBN: 0395709407
  • This breakthrough book puts the ecology back into gardening. It describes basic components of natural ecosystems, explains their benefits and their fragility, and urges gardeners to design landscapes that are closer to their local pre-settlement ones. Stein champions "wild gardening" as a way to create lower maintenance, more natural-looking landscapes and at the same time preserve native species of plants and animals.

Stein, Sara. Planting Noah's Garden: Further Adventures in Backyard Ecology (Houghton Mifflin, 1997). ISBN: 0395709601
  • By popular demand, Stein wrote this sequel to Noah's Garden. It lays out steps for injecting "wildness" into your yard, whether you live in the city, suburbs, town, or country. Stein explains how to accomplish major projects—find and start a group of wild gardeners, order plants wholesale, plant large quantities quickly and effectively, and

create different types of natural communities (woodland, wetland, grassland)—but doesn't neglect the details like moving heavy rocks, sowing wild seeds, do-it-yourself soil analysis, and more. A thorough and instructive guide that contains many motivational stories and color photos.

Stewart, Amy. <u>From the Ground Up: The Story of a First Garden</u> (St. Martin's Press, 2002). ISBN: 0312287674
- This book captures the coming of age of a gentle and thoughtful gardener. Stewart describes her mistakes and discoveries as a young gardener in a small town lot in southern California.

Stokes, Donald; **Lillian Stokes**; and **Ernest Williams**. <u>The Butterfly Book</u> (Little, Brown, 1991). ISBN: 0316817805
- Great beginner's guide to main species of butterfly and what plants they use and their ranges through North America. Includes color photos of both butterfly and caterpillar stage for each species. Also offers general discussion of some butterfly behaviors such as puddling.

Tanner, Ogden. <u>Living Fences : A Gardener's Guide to Hedges, Vines & Espaliers</u> (Chapters, 1995). ISBN: 1881527689
- Good in-depth overview of ways to use plants as barriers—for privacy, beauty, or to delineate spaces. Covers hedges (shorn and unshorn), vines, and espaliers. Describes plant species for each type of barrier, over 100 total species.

Tekiela, Stan. <u>Birds of Minnesota Field Guide</u>. (Adventure Publications: 2nd edition, 2004) ISBN: 1591930375
- Devotes two pages to each of the bird species that lives in or regularly passes through Minnesota. Includes color photo, physical description, nesting and mating and young-rearing specifics. Describes call and range as well as when and where to find each species.

Thompson, Peter. <u>The Self-Sustaining Garden : A Gardener's Guide to Matrix Planting</u>. (Trafalgar Square, 1997) ISBN: 0713481331
- Explores techniques for planting gardens that will endure with minimal or no care once established. Discusses "matrix" planting (knitting together more decorative specimens with abundant numbers of a background or matrix plant) and choosing plants appropriate to the conditions of the landscape.

Van Melle, Peter J. <u>Shrubs and Trees for the Small Place: Hardy Deciduous Materials for the Home Grounds</u>. (Doubleday: Revised edition, 1955) ASIN: B00005XW3D

- Now out-of-print. Useful not only for descriptions and comparisons of various shrub and tree species appropriate for small gardens, but also for Van Melle's method of rating plants according to garden design criteria.

Verey, Rosemary. <u>The Art of Planting</u>. (Little, Brown: 1st North American edition, 1990) ISBN: 0316899763

- Verey's book is replete with instructional stories that draw on her vast experience to examine the art of combining plants for all-season beauty and compatible growth habits. Detailed discussion and color photos illuminate the visual qualities of plants - shape, density, texture, color, and so forth.

Williams, Bunny with **Nancy Drew**. <u>On Garden Style</u>. (Simon & Schuster, 1998) ISBN: 0684826054

- Award-winning interior designer Williams explores many aspects of designing an artistic and tasteful landscape. The book doesn't focus on particular plants, but rather on different sensory and structural contributions that plants and other elements (from containers to passageways) can make to a design.

Williams, Carol. <u>Bringing a Garden to Life</u>. (Bantam, 1998) ISBN: 055309680-X

- Down-to-earth advice on maintaining a garden over time, written in a sure and poetic voice. Discusses how plants grow—their behaviors and life cycles—and how gardeners can work with the knowledge of these natural processes to make healthy and beautiful gardens.

Williams, Robin. <u>Garden Design: How to Be Your Own Landscape Architect</u>. (Readers Digest, 1995) ISBN: 0895776766

- This practical sourcebook presents stylistic options for different elements of garden design, such as steps, fences and walls, and water features. Includes structural answers to many design challenges such as addressing poor drainage, choosing focal points, and integrating entertainment and game-playing areas into the garden. Provides a broad, basic introduction to garden design possibilities.

Author's Note: Latin names for trees and shrubs were verified using sources from the above list (most often, Hightshoe). Latin names for perennials and annuals, particularly cultivars, were verified using <u>The American Horticultural Society's A-Z Encyclopedia of Plants</u>, edited by Christopher Brickell and Judith D. Zuk and published by DK in 1997.

Index

Y

Z